Editor
Sara Connolly

Editor in Chief
Ina Massler Levin, M.A.

Creative Director
Karen J. Goldfluss, M.S. Ed.

Cover Artist
Brenda DiAntonis

Imaging
Leonard P. Swierski

Publisher

Mary D. Smith, M.S. Ed.

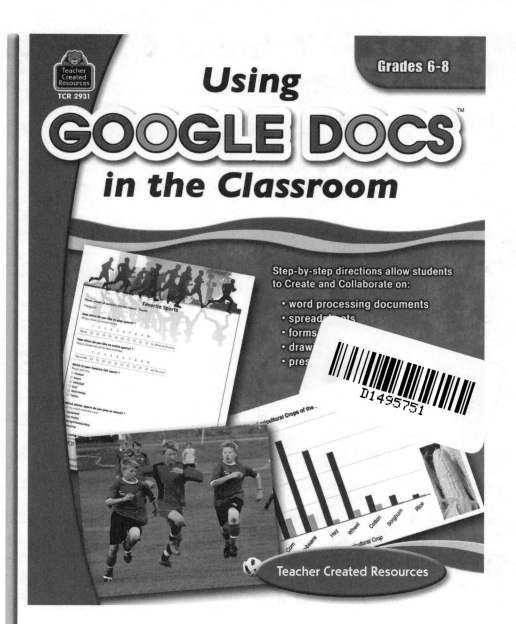

Grades 6-8

TCR 2931

Using
GOOGLE DOCS™
in the Classroom

Step-by-step directions allow students to Create and Collaborate on:

- word processing documents
- spreadsheets
- forms
- drawings
- presentations

Teacher Created Resources

Author

Steve Butz

Teacher Created Resources
6421 Industry Way
Westminster, CA 92683
www.teachercreated.com

ISBN: 978-1-4206-2931-6

©2012 Teacher Created Resources
Reprinted, 2014
Made in U.S.A.

Teacher Created Resources

Table of Contents

Introduction. 3

Google Docs™ and Collaboration 4

Word Processing Activities

Activity 1: Formatting Drill. 5

Activity 2: Book Report 11

Activity 3: A Famous American's Social Media Page 16

Spreadsheet Activities

Activity 4: Exploration Timeline. 26

Activity 5: Electricity Cost Calculator 31

Activity 6: Major Crops of the United States 36

Activity 7: Climographs 40

Activity 8: What's in Seawater? 45

Activity 9: Human Population Growth 50

Drawing Activities

Activity 10: National Weather Map. 54

Activity 11: Technological Systems Diagram 62

Form Activities

Activity 12: Favorite Book, Movie, and TV Show Survey. 72

Activity 13: Popular Sports Survey. 77

Presentation Activities

Activity 14: Favorite Animal. 83

Activity 15: Invasive Species. 89

Introduction

Using Google Docs in the Classroom was written for teachers who would like to utilize the Google Docs™ program to enhance their curriculum. Google Docs is a free online software suite that gives students access to word processing, spreadsheet, presentation, and drawing programs. With Google Docs, students can create, edit, share, and collaborate on documents with their peers. All files are stored by Google and are accessible from any computer that has Internet access, giving students the opportunity to continue to work on their school projects from home. The only requirement for use is an email address. (If your students do not have email addresses, contact your school's technology coordinator to discuss ways to provide free email solutions for your students.)

The activities in this book were designed for use in a computer lab or classroom setting where students have access to online computers. Each activity has been successfully used in the classroom and was designed to be completed in a forty-five minute computer lab session. Each activity includes the overall purpose of the lesson, learning objectives, materials required, and detailed step-by-step procedures, along with informative pictures that show you exactly what to do. No knowledge of software applications is required to teach the activities contained in this book.

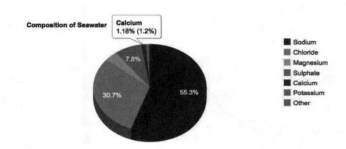

The book is arranged in five sections that correlate to the five different types of software applications available in Google Docs: Word Processing, Spreadsheets, Drawings, Forms, and Presentations. The 15 activities contained in this book address many different ways in which educators can utilize software. This offers teachers the opportunity to confidently take classes into the computer lab and use Google Docs to present a well-rounded lesson.

Although each lesson contains specific subject matter, all labs in this book can be easily adapted to fit your specific lesson plans by using your own data. The labs are designed to illustrate the many ways that computers can be used in your classroom to reinforce your specific topic of study, and may provide you with a variety of ways to incorporate technology into your curriculum.

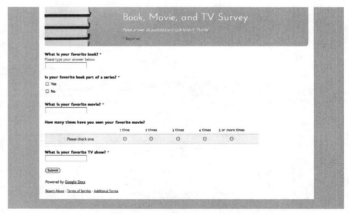

Get started with Google Docs by going to **http://docs.google.com**. Sign in with your Google account, or click on **create an account now** to sign up using your email address.

Google Docs™ and Collaboration

One of the advantages of using the Google Docs program is that it provides students with a method of collaborating on projects. What this means is that students can grant specified people access to their online documents. This access can allow others to either read or edit documents. If you grant edit permission to a document, then students can work on the same document simultaneously. This is especially useful for group projects using presentation software. Students can grant others access to their documents by clicking the link to the **Sharing Settings**. (See Figure A.)

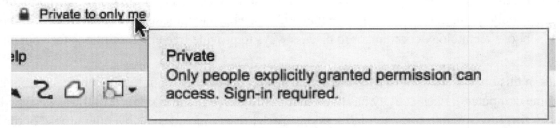

Figure A

Under the Sharing Settings window, you can add the email addresses of people you wish to either view or edit your documents. Select **Can view** or **Can edit** depending on what you would like them to be able to do. You can also send them an email that provides a link to access your document. (See Figure B.)

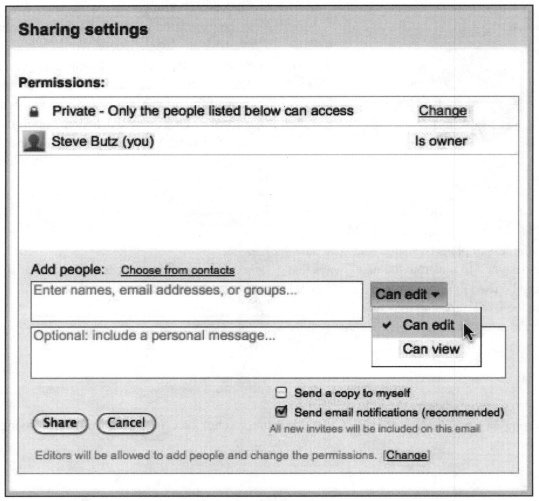

Figure B

Formatting Drill

Activity 1

Objectives

Each student will utilize the Google Docs word processing application to edit and format a document.

Benchmarks for Technology Standards

Students will know the characteristics, uses, and basic features of computer software programs, including:

- opening a file
- applying formatting to text
- editing, copying, moving, and saving text
- formatting text by centering lines, using tabs, and by forming paragraphs
- changing the line spacing of text

Learning Objectives

At the end of this lesson, students will be able to:

1. insert and align text in a document
2. change the font of text in a document
3. change font size, style, and color
4. change the line spacing of a paragraph
5. create a bulleted list
6. insert a line into a document
7. insert an image into a document

Variations

This activity was written using the processes that together make up the water cycle; however, any cyclical process can be substituted. An example of a completed document is shown in Figure 1-1.

Formatting Drill *(cont.)*

Word Processing

Activity 1

The Water Cycle

The water cycle begins when water from the ocean is heated by the sun and ***evaporates*** into the atmosphere as water vapor.

The water vapor rises up, cools, and ***condenses*** to form clouds and ***precipitation***.

Precipitation, in the form of rain and snow, returns to the surface where it can collect in ponds and lakes, run off into streams and rivers, or enter the ground.

Infiltration is the process of water entering the ground and becoming ***groundwater***.

Groundwater can then be taken up by roots, moved up through a plant, and evaporated off the leaf surface in a process known as ***evapotranspiration***.

Figure 1-1

Formatting Drill (cont.)

Activity 1

Procedure

1. Sign in to Google Docs.
2. Go to **Create** and choose **Document**.
3. Click into the **Untitled document** box at the upper left corner of the page and type in your last name, then "Water Cycle" (Figure 1-2). Click **OK** in the **Rename Document** window.

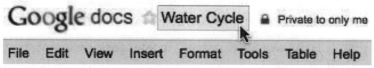

Figure 1-2

4. Next, type in the following title into your document: "The Water Cycle."
5. Now highlight the title and center it by using the **Center align** button. (See Figure 1-3.)

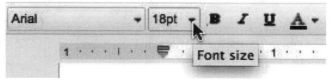

Figure 1-3

6. Next, keep the title highlighted and increase its font size to **18** using the **Font size** button. Also make the title bold and underlined by using the **Bold** button (**B**) and the **Underline** button (**U**) (Figure 1-4).

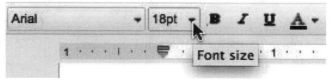

Figure 1-4

7. Click away from the title, then hit the **Enter** key on your keyboard twice. This will take you down two lines. Type in the following sentence: "The water cycle begins when water from the ocean is heated by the sun and evaporates into the atmosphere as water vapor."
8. Highlight the sentence by clicking and dragging over it. Click the **Bold** button (**B**) and the **Underline** button (**U**) to remove the bold and underline formatting. Then change the font size to **14** and the font to **Cambria** using the **Font** menu (Figure 1-5).

Figure 1-5

Formatting Drill (cont.)

Activity 1

9. With your sentence still highlighted, use the **Left align** button to align your sentence to the left margin (Figure 1-6).

Figure 1-6

10. Next, click and highlight only the word "evaporates" in your paragraph. Increase its font size to **18**, and use the **Italics** (*I*) and **Bold** (**B**) buttons to change its format to italics and bold (Figure 1-7).

The Water Cycle

The water cycle begins when water from the ocean is heated by the sun and ***evaporates*** into the atmosphere as water vapor.

Figure 1-7

11. While the word is still highlighted, change its color to **blue** using the **Text color** button (Figure 1-8).

Figure 1-8

12. Now click at the end of the sentence, hit the **Enter** key twice, and type "The water vapor rises up, cools, and condenses to form clouds and precipitation."

13. Highlight this sentence, and use the **Right align** button to align it to the right side of the page.

14. Click and highlight the word "condenses" in your paragraph. Increase its font size to **18**, and use the **Italics** (*I*) and **Bold** buttons (**B**) to change its format to italics and bold. Also change its color to **blue**.

15. Repeat steps 13 and 14 for the word "precipitation" (Figure 1-9).

The Water Cycle

The water cycle begins when water from the ocean is heated by the sun and ***evaporates*** into the atmosphere as water vapor.

The water vapor rises up, cools, and ***condenses*** to form clouds and ***precipitation***.

Figure 1-9

16. Click at the end of the sentence, hit the **Enter** key twice, then type "Precipitation, in the form of rain and snow, returns to the surface where it can collect in ponds and lakes, run off into streams and rivers, or enter the ground."

17. Now you are going to use the justify command. Justify makes your paragraph align to both the left and right margins of your page, making your text appear like a box. This is a common alignment used in books, magazines, and newspapers. Highlight the sentence and click the **Justify** button (Figure 1-10).

The Water Cycle

Figure 1-10

18. Next, highlight the word "Precipitation," increase its font size to **18**, also format it so that it is in **Bold**, **Italics**, and the color **blue**.

19. Click to the end of the third paragraph, hit the **Enter** key twice, and type "Infiltration is the process of water entering the ground and becoming groundwater."

20. Change the font size to **18**, **Bold**, and **Italics** for the words "Infiltration" and "groundwater." Also change their color to **blue** (Figure 1-11).

Infiltration **is the process of water entering the ground and becoming** ***groundwater***.

Figure 1-11

21. Click to the end of the fourth paragraph, hit the **Enter** key twice, and type in the following: "Groundwater can then be taken up by roots, moved up through a plant, and evaporated off the leaf surface in a process known as evapotranspiration."

22. Highlight the word "evapotranspiration" and change its font size to **18**, **Bold**, and **Italics**. Also change its color to **blue**.

23. Click and drag over the entire paragraph. Click the **Left align** button.

24. Next, click and drag over all five paragraphs to highlight them. Change their line spacing to **1.0** using the **Line spacing** button (Figure 1-12).

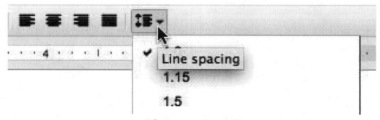

Figure 1-12

Formatting Drill *(cont.)*

Activity 1

25. Click after the last sentence of the last paragraph. Then hit the **Enter** key twice to move you down two line spaces. You will now enter a horizontal line into your document to act as a dividing line. To do this, select the **Insert** menu and choose **Horizontal line** (Figure 1-13).

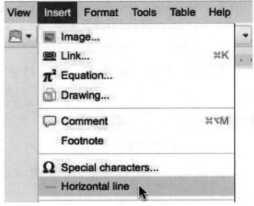

Figure 1-13

26. Your project is now complete!

Book Report

Activity 2

Objectives

Each student will use the Google Docs word processing application to create a template that he or she can use to prepare a book report.

Benchmarks for Technology Standards

Students will know the characteristics, uses, and basic features of computer software programs, including:

- using the common features of desktop publishing and word processing software
- knowing that documents can be created, designed, and formatted
- using a word processor to print text

Learning Objectives

At the end of this lesson, students will be able to:

1. create a new word processing document
2. enter text into a document
3. format font size and style
4. change the font of text in a document
5. alter the color of a font
6. use keyboard commands to format text
7. add page numbers to a document
8. create a copy of a document

Before the Computer

Before you begin this assignment, make sure each student has the following information about a book he or she recently read: title, author, publisher, date published, and number of pages. An example of a completed document is shown in Figure 2-1.

Book Report
by Steve Butz

Title:
Author:
Publisher:
Year Published:
Number of Pages:

Book Summary (please include characters, setting, main events, etc.):

Figure 2-1

Book Report *(cont.)*
Activity 2

Procedure

1. Sign in to Google Docs.

2. Go to **Create** and choose **Document**.

3. In the **Untitled Document** box at the upper-left corner of the page, type your last name and "Book Report Template." (See Figure 2-2.) Click **OK** in the **Rename Document** window.

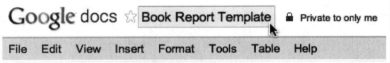

Figure 2-2

4. Type the following title at the top of your document: "Book Report." Highlight the title by clicking and dragging over it. Then center it by clicking on the **Center align** icon. Your title should now be centered.

5. Increase the font size of your title by clicking on the **Font size** button and selecting **24 pt**. Click on the **Font** menu to change the font to **Cambria** (Figure 2-3).

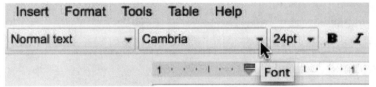

Figure 2-3

6. Next, hit **Enter** on your keyboard, type "by," and then type your first name and last name. Highlight your name and reduce its font size to **14 pt** (Figure 2-4).

Book Report
by Steve Butz
Figure 2-4

7. Hit the **Enter** key twice to move down two lines. Click the **Left align** button to move your cursor to the left margin (Figure 2-5).

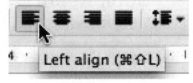

Figure 2-5

8. Now type "Title." Hit the **Colon** key on your keyboard (:).

9. Next, highlight just the word "Title" (not the colon) and use the **Bold** (**B**) and **Underline** (<u>U</u>) buttons to make the word bold and underlined (Figure 2-6).

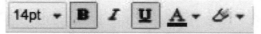

Figure 2-6

10. You can also use your keyboard to change the style of text to bold or underlined. If you are using a Macintosh computer, hold down the **Command** and **B** keys on your keyboard to make your text bold. For a PC, use the **Control** and **B** keys. To underline text, use the **Command** and **U** keys or **Control** and **U** keys (Figure 2-7).

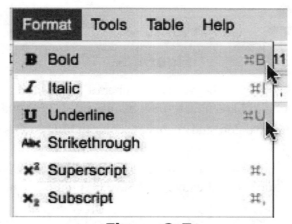

Figure 2-7

11. With your text still highlighted, use the **Text color** button to change the color of the text to **blue** (Figure 2-8).

Figure 2-8

12. Next, hit the **Enter** key once, type "Author," and hit the **Colon** key. Repeat steps 9–11 to format the text.

13. Add the following information to your document so that it looks like Figure 2-9.

Book Report

by Steve Butz

<u>**Title**</u>:
<u>**Author**</u>:
<u>**Publisher**</u>:
<u>**Year Published**</u>:
<u>**Number of Pages**</u>:

Figure 2-9

14. Now click after the colon that follows the words "Number of Pages" and hit the **Enter** key twice. Type "Book Summary (please include characters, setting, main events, etc.)" and hit the **Colon** key.

15. Highlight the text, excluding the colon, and change its color to **blue** and its style to **Bold** (**B**) and **Underlined** (<u>**U**</u>).

16. Your book report template is now complete. Make sure to click the **Save Now** button located in the upper-right corner of your page if it does not already read "Saved" (Figure 2-10).

Figure 2-10

17. Next, you will use your template to create your first book report.

18. Go to the **File** menu and choose **Make a copy...** (Figure 2-11).

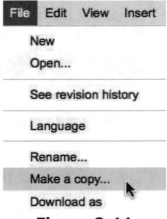

Figure 2-11

19. In the **Copy Document** window, click **OK**. A copy of your book report template will open in a new window. Click into the **Document Name** box (Figure 2-12). The **Copy Document** window will come up. Click **OK**.

Figure 2-12

20. In the **Rename Document** window, change the file name to your last name and the title of your book (Figure 2-13).

Figure 2-13

21. Click **OK**. Now you can enter the information for your first book report, which includes title, author, publisher, year published, number of pages, and a brief summary.

22. When all the information for your book is completed, and your book report is finished, you can add page numbers to it and print it.

23. Go to the **Insert** menu and choose **Page numbers**. Select **Bottom of page** from the menu (Figure 2-14).

Figure 2-14

24. Go to the **File** menu and select **Print**. Click the **Print** button. Your project is now complete!

A Famous American's Social Media Page

Activity 3

Objectives

Each student will use the Google Docs word processing application to create a mock social media page for a famous American.

Benchmarks for Technology Standards

Students will know the characteristics, uses, and basic features of computer software programs, including:

- using the common features of desktop publishing and word processing software
- knowing that documents can be created, designed, and formatted
- using a word processor to print text

Learning Objectives

At the end of this lesson, students will be able to:

1. create a new word processing document
2. enter text into a document
3. format font size and style
4. change the font of text in a document
5. alter the color of a font
6. insert and format an image into a document
7. adjust the indent of a document
8. insert a drawing and a text box into a document
9. change the alignment of text within a text box
10. insert a horizontal line into a document
11. change the position of an image within a document
12. insert word art into a document
13. insert special characters into a document
14. print a document

Before the Computer

This assignment uses the biography of Rosa Parks, a civil rights icon who helped changed the segregation laws in the United States by using nonviolent protest. After students complete this assignment, you may wish to assign them to create their own mock social media page for their own famous American. An example of a completed document is shown in Figure 3-1.

A Famous American's Social Media Page *(cont.)*

Activity 3

Rosa Parks

Home   Friends' Pages   Create Your Page   About

☆ Born on February 4, 1913 in Tuskegee, Alabama

☆ Attended Miss White's School for Girls, Montgomery Industrial School for Girls, and Alabama State Teachers College

☆ Employed as an aide to Congressman John Conyers

☆ With her husband Raymond, founded the Rosa and Raymond Parks Institute for Self Development

Write your message for Rosa Parks here.

Representative Julia Carson
Rosa, you have just been awarded the Congressional Medal of Honor!
May 3, 1999

President William Clinton
Congratulations on receiving the Medal of Freedom, Rosa!
September 1996

Congressman John Conyers
Rosa, thank you for your hard work as my congressional aide from 1965 to 1988!
July 1988

Dr. Martin Luther King, Jr.
Thank you, Rosa, for your nonviolent stance against racial segregation.
December 1955

Figure 3-1

A Famous American's Social Media Page *(cont.)*

Activity 3

Procedure

1. Sign in to Google Docs.
2. Go to **Create** and choose **Document**. Click into the **Untitled document** box to bring up the **Rename Document** window. Type your last name and then "Rosa Parks Social Media Bio." Click **OK**.
3. Next, go to the **Insert** menu and choose **Drawing** to bring up the drawing window.
4. Select the **Actions** menu (Figure 3-2).

Figure 3-2

5. Select the **Word Art** option, which looks like a "T."

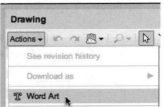

Figure 3-3

6. In the text box, type "Rosa Parks," then hit the **Enter** key on your keyboard.
7. Next, change the font to **Georgia** using the **Font** menu (Figure 3-4).

Figure 3-4

8. Now you will change the color of your word art. Click the **Fill color** button (Figure 3-5) and choose the color **Green RGB (56, 118, 29)** (Figure 3-6).

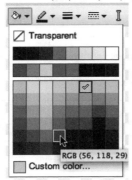

Figure 3-5

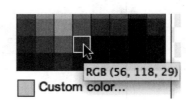

Figure 3-6

A Famous American's Social Media Page *(cont.)*

Activity 3

9. Next, use the **Line Color** button to change the line color of your word art to the same green that you used for the fill (Figure 3-7).

Figure 3-7

10. Your word art is now ready to be inserted into your document. Hit the **Save & Close** button (Figure 3-8).

Figure 3-8

11. The word art should now appear in your document. You may need to make it smaller to fit within the boundaries of the page. Click and drag the lower-right anchor point of the word art to resize it. Click and drag the word art itself to center it on the page.

12. Now return to the **Insert** menu and choose **Drawing** once again. In the **Drawing** window, select the **Text box** tool (Figure 3-9).

Figure 3-9

13. Draw a text box that is 3 grid-squares high and about 38 grid-squares wide (Figure 3-10).

Figure 3-10

14. Type "Home" in the text box. Hit the **Space bar** on your keyboard five times, then type "Friends' Pages." Hit the **Space bar** five more times, then type "Create Your Page." Hit the **Space bar** five more times, then type "About" (Figure 3-11). Then hit the **Enter** key.

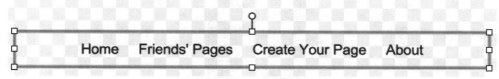

Figure 3-11

A Famous American's Social Media Page *(cont.)*

Activity 3

15. Next, use the **Text color** menu to change the color of the text to **white** (Figure 3-12).

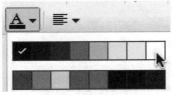

Figure 3-12

16. Now change the line and fill colors to the same green you used for your word art. Click the **Save & Close** button to insert the text box.

17. Your document should now look like the one in Figure 3-13.

Figure 3-13

18. Next, you will insert a line to separate your document. Hit the **Enter** key on your keyboard, then select the **Insert** menu and choose **Horizontal line**.

19. Hit the **Enter** key once again to take you down one line. Now you will insert an image into your document.

20. Go to the **Insert** menu and choose **Image**. In the **Insert image** window, choose **Google Image Search**, and type "Rosa Parks" in the **Search images** box. Click the **Search images** button. Scroll down and click on an image of Rosa Parks, and click the **Select** button (Figure 3-14).

Figure 3-14

21. The image should now be inserted into your document. Click on it to highlight it, then grab the bottom-right anchor point and click and drag the image to reduce its size (Figure 3-15).

Figure 3-15

A Famous American's Social Media Page *(cont.)*

Activity 3

22. With the image still selected, click **Fixed position** in the box below the image (Figure 3-16).

Figure 3-16

23. Now click your cursor to the top-left of the picture (Figure 3-17).

Figure 3-17

24. Next, click on the **Left Indent** tool and drag it to the **2 1/4 inch** mark on the ruler (Figure 3-18). This will make your left indent start at the right side of the image.

Figure 3-18

25. Hit the **Enter** key once to bring your cursor down, then reduce the font size to **11 pt**.

26. Now you will insert a special character. Go to the **Insert** menu and choose **Special characters** (Figure 3-19).

Insert	Format	Tools	Table	Help

- Image...
- Link... ⌘K
- π^2 Equation...
- Drawing...
- Comment ⌘⌥M
- Footnote
- Ω Special characters...
- — Horizontal line

Figure 3-19

27. In the **Insert Special Characters** window, click on the **Arrows** drop-down menu and select **Stars/Asterisks** (Figure 3-20).

Figure 3-20

Activity 3

28. Scroll down the list of special characters until you find a star you like (Figure 3-21), then click on it and click **OK** to insert it into your document.

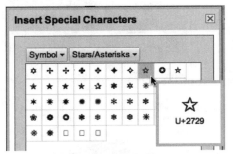

Figure 3-21

29. Now type in the following information about Rosa Parks, hitting the **Enter** key twice after every line and inserting the special character star when needed: "☆ Born on February 4, 1913 in Tuskegee, Alabama ☆ Attended Miss White's School for Girls, Montgomery Industrial School for Girls, and Alabama State Teachers College ☆ Employed as an aide to Congressman John Conyers ☆ With her husband Raymond, founded the Rosa and Raymond Parks Institute for Self Development" (Figure 3-22).

☆ Born on February 4, 1913 in Tuskegee, Alabama

☆ Attended Miss White's School for Girls, Montgomery Industrial School for Girls, and Alabama State Teachers College

☆ Employed as an aide to Congressman John Conyers

☆ With her husband Raymond, founded the Rosa and Raymond Parks Institute for Self Development

Figure 3-22

30. Next, hit the **Enter** key enough times to bring your cursor down to just below the picture. Then click and drag the **Left Indent** tool back to the left margin again.

31. Now insert another horizontal line. Go to the **Insert** menu and choose **Horizontal line**. Then hit the **Enter** key again to bring your cursor down one line.

32. Go to the **Insert** menu, and choose **Drawing**. In the drawing window, use the **Text box** tool to draw a text box 3 grid squares high and about 38 grid squares wide.

33. In your text box, type "Write your message for Rosa Parks here." Hit the **Enter** key, and change the font color of the text box to **gray RGB (153, 153, 153)**. Change the line color to the same green you used before. Then hit the **Save & Close** button to insert the text box into your document.

34. Click your cursor just to the right of the text box, then hit the **Enter** key once to bring you down one line.

35. Now you are going to add some comments from people who were associated with Rosa Parks. This will be used to illustrate important events in the life of Rosa Parks.

A Famous American's Social Media Page *(cont.)*

Activity 3

36. First you will insert an image of the person. Another way to insert an image is using Google's image search to locate an image, then you can just click and drag it in to your slide. To do this, go to the **File** menu of your web browser and choose **New Window** (Figure 3-23).

Figure 3-23

37. Next, navigate to the following web address, **http://www.google.com**. Click the **Image search** link at the top of the page, then type "Congresswoman Julia Carson" into the **Search Images** box and hit the **Search** button.

38. Your image search should have produced many images of Julia Carson. Click the bottom corner of your web browser to minimize it so it takes up only half of your screen. Then click and drag an image of Julia Carson onto your slide (Figure 3-24).

Figure 3-24

39. Your image should now be inserted into your slide. Click on the image to highlight it, and grab the anchor point on the lower right to reduce its size so it is about the size of a postage stamp (Figure 3-25).

Figure 3-25

Activity 3

40. Next, with the image still highlighted, click **Fixed position** in the box below the picture. This will fix the location in your document so it does not move with the text. Now click just to the upper left of the image to place your cursor near the left margin (Figure 3-26).

Figure 3-26

41. Now click and drag the **Left Indent** tool (Figure 3-27) to set the margin to **1 inch**.

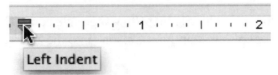

Figure 3-27

42. Now your margin will be aligned just to the right of the picture. Next, type "Representative Julia Carson," then hit **Enter** on your keyboard to bring you down one line. Now type "Rosa, you have just been awarded the Congressional Medal of Honor!"

43. Hit the **Enter** key again and type "May 3, 1999." Finally, hit the **Enter** key about four times to bring your cursor down below the picture. Use the **Left Indent** tool to reset the indent back to the left margin (Figure 3-28).

Figure 3-28

44. Now change the font color of Representative Carson's name to the same green color you used before, and the date to the same gray color you used before (Figure 3-29).

Representative Julia Carson
Rosa, you have just been awarded the Congressional Medal of Honor!
May 3, 1999

Figure 3-29

A Famous American's Social Media Page *(cont.)*

Activity 3

45. Click back down below Mrs. Carson's picture. You will now repeat Steps 36–44 to add more comments about important events that occurred in the life of Rosa Parks, as shown in Figure 3-30.

Representative Julia Carson
Rosa, you have just been awarded the Congressional Medal of Honor!
May 3, 1999

President William Clinton
Congratulations on receiving the Medal of Freedom, Rosa!
September 1996

Congressman John Conyers
Rosa, thank you for your hard work as my congressional aide from 1965 to 1988!
July 1988

Dr. Martin Luther King, Jr.
Thank you, Rosa, for your nonviolent stance against racial segregation.
December 1955

Figure 3-30

46. Your project is now complete!

Exploration Timeline

Activity 4

Objectives

Each student will use the Google Docs spreadsheet application to create a timeline of exploration.

Benchmarks for Technology Standards

Students will know the characteristics, uses, and basic features of computer software programs, including:

- using the common features of spreadsheets
- using spreadsheet software to update, add, and delete data, and to produce charts

Learning Objectives

At the end of this lesson, students will be able to:

1. know the various terms associated with spreadsheets, including rows, columns, and cells

2. enter data into a spreadsheet

3. adjust the width of a selected column

4. change the alignment of data within a cell

5. change the style of data within a cell

6. format the background color of a cell

7. add a border around a cell

8. sort data within a column

Variations

Although this activity uses the dates and names associated with exploration, a spreadsheet can be created for any timeline. An example of a completed project is shown in Figure 4-1.

Date	Explorer
1000	Leif Erickson explores North American coast.
1275	Marco Polo begins exploration of China.
1341	Ibn Battuta begins exploration of India and China.
1405	Zheng He explores Indian Ocean and East African coast.
1492	Christoper Columbus sails to the Caribbean.
1497	John Cabot explores the coast of Newfoundland.
1497	Vasco da Gama sails to India around the southern tip of Africa.
1499	Amerigo Vespucci maps east coast of South America.
1513	Vasco Nunez de Balboa crosses Panama and arrives at the Pacific Ocean.
1513	Ponce de Leon explores Florida.
1519	Ferdinand Magellan sails around the globe.
1524	Giovanni da Verrazzano explores North American coast.
1541	Jacques Cartier explores Canada and the St. Lawrence River.
1609	Samuel de Champlain explores Great Lakes region of North America.
1609	Henry Hudson sails up the Hudson River.

Figure 4-1

Exploration Timeline (cont.)

Activity 4

Procedure

1. Open a new spreadsheet document.

2. In the **Unsaved spreadsheet** box, type your last name and then "Explorer Timeline." Click **OK** in the **Save Spreadsheet** window.

3. Spreadsheets are made up of columns that are identified by letters (A, B, C, etc.) and rows that are identified by numbers (1, 2, 3, etc.).

4. The location within a spreadsheet where a column meets a row is called a *cell*, and is identified by both a letter and number (Figure 4-2).

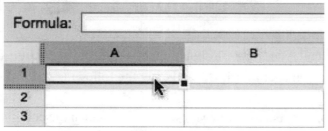

Figure 4-2

5. Type in the following title into cell **A1**: "Date."

6. Next, hit the **Tab** key on your keyboard. This will move you over one cell to the right, into cell **B1**. Now type in "Explorer."

7. Hit the **Enter** key on your keyboard. This will take you down one cell. Now click and drag over both cells **A1** and **B1** to highlight them.

8. Click the **Align** button, and choose the option to center the text in each cell (Figure 4-3).

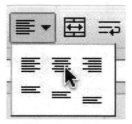

Figure 4-3

9. Also use the **Bold (B)** button to make your titles bold (Figure 4-4).

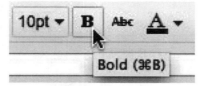

Figure 4-4

Exploration Timeline *(cont.)*

Activity 4

10. Now you will change the background color of the cells. With cells **A1** and **B1** still highlighted, choose the **Text background color** button (Figure 4-5) and change the color to **light blue**.

Figure 4-5

11. Next, click into cell **A2** and type "1000." Center the date by using the **Align Center** button.

12. Hit the **Tab** key to move you over to cell **B2**, and enter the following text: "**Leif Ericson explores North American coast**."

13. Hit the **Enter** key on your keyboard. Now you will have to widen the column for the text to fit on only one line. To do this, click in between columns B and C, and drag it to the right until the entire sentence fits (Figure 4-6).

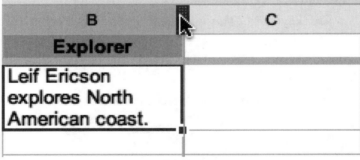

Figure 4-6

14. Next, click into cell **A3** and type in the following year: "1275." Hit the **Tab** key on your keyboard to move you over to cell **B3**. Now type "Marco Polo begins exploration of China." Make sure the year is centered in its cell.

Exploration Timeline (cont.)

Spreadsheets

Activity 4

15. Now continue to fill out your timeline by using the following information:

Date	Explorer
1341	Ibn Battuta begins exploration of India and China.
1541	Jacques Cartier explores Canada and the St. Lawrence River.
1609	Samuel de Champlain explores Great Lakes region of North America.
1405	Zheng He explores Indian Ocean and East African coast.
1524	Giovanni da Verrazzano explores North American coast.
1492	Christopher Columbus sails to the Caribbean.
1513	Vasco Nunez de Balboa crosses Panama and arrives at the Pacific Ocean.
1499	Amerigo Vespucci maps east coast of South America.
1513	Ponce de Leon explores Florida.
1497	John Cabot explores the coast of Newfoundland.
1519	Ferdinand Magellan sails around the globe.
1609	Henry Hudson sails up Hudson River.
1497	Vasco da Gama sails to India around the southern tip of Africa.

16. Once all of your information has been entered, make sure all the dates are centered, the explorer information is aligned to the left, and your column B is wide enough (Figure 4-7).

Date	Explorer
1000	Leif Erickson explores North American coast.
1275	Marco Polo begins exploration of China.
1341	Ibn Battuta begins exploration of India and China.
1405	Zheng He explores Indian Ocean and East African coast.
1492	Christoper Columbus sails to the Caribbean.
1497	John Cabot explores the coast of Newfoundland.
1497	Vasco da Gama sails to India around the southern tip of Africa.
1499	Amerigo Vespucci maps east coast of South America.
1513	Vasco Nunez de Balboa crosses Panama and arrives at the Pacific Ocean.
1513	Ponce de Leon explores Florida.
1519	Ferdinand Magellan sails around the globe.
1524	Giovanni da Verrazzano explores North American coast.
1541	Jacques Cartier explores Canada and the St. Lawrence River.
1609	Samuel de Champlain explores Great Lakes region of North America.
1609	Henry Hudson sails up the Hudson River.

Figure 4-7

Exploration Timeline (cont.)

Activity 4

17. Next, you are going to add borders around each cell within your spreadsheet. To do this, highlight all of your timeline information by clicking and dragging over it. Then click the **Borders** button and choose the option for adding a border all around each cell (Figure 4-8).

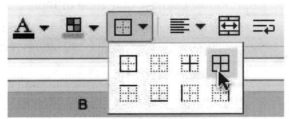

Figure 4-8

18. Finally, you will use the **Sort** command to sort your timeline by the date. To do this, highlight just the dates in column A by clicking and dragging over them. Then choose the **Data** menu and select **Sort Range . . . .** Click in the box beside **Data has header row**. Then select **Sort sheet by column A, A-Z** (Figure 4-9).

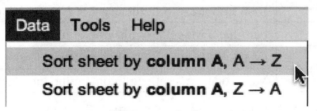

Figure 4-9

19. You can also sort your data within a column by moving your cursor to the top of Column A, and clicking on the small arrow on the right to bring up the **Column Menu** (Figure 4-10). Then choose the **Sort sheet A-Z** option.

A	
Date	Cut
1000	Copy
1275	
1341	Paste
1541	Paste **values** only
1609	Paste **format** only
1405	
1524	Insert 1 left
1492	Insert 1 right
1513	
1499	Delete column
1513	Clear column
1497	Hide column
1519	
1609	Resize column...
1497	
	Sort sheet A → Z
	Sort sheet Z → A

Figure 4-10

20. Your dates should now be in order, and your timeline project is complete and ready to be printed!

Electricity Cost Calculator

Activity 5

Objectives

Each student will use Google Docs spreadsheet application to create a spreadsheet that will calculate the cost of operating standard household appliances.

Benchmarks for Technology Standards

Students will know the characteristics, uses, and basic features of computer software programs, including:

- using the common features of spreadsheets
- using spreadsheet software to update, add, and delete data, and to produce charts

Learning Objectives

At the end of this lesson, students will be able to:

1. know the various terms associated with spreadsheets, including rows, columns, and cells
2. enter data into a spreadsheet
3. adjust the width of a selected column
4. change the alignment of data within a cell
5. enter a mathematical formula into a cell
6. insert a function into a cell
7. format the background color of a cell
8. change the format of numbers within a cell
9. change the rounding of numbers within a cell

Before the Computer

This activity provides the amount of hours each day that specific appliances are used. To make this activity more realistic, ask your students to gather information about how many hours per day some of their appliances at home are used. Students can also perform an Internet search to find the average watts required to run standard appliances that they might have in their homes. Also, this activity uses the national average cost of electricity, which is approximately 11 cents per kilowatt hour. You can look online on your local energy provider's website to find the average rate in your area and substitute it in this activity. An example of a completed project is shown in Figure 5-1.

	A	B	C	D	E	F
	Appliance	**Hours/Day Used**	**Watts**	**Watt Hours**	**Kilowatt Hours**	**Cost of Use**
	26-inch LCD TV	5	110	550	0.55	$0.06
	Window Fan	10	150	1500	1.5	$0.17
	Personal Computer	5	125	625	0.625	$0.07
	Totals	**20**	**385**	**2675**	**2.675**	**$0.29**

Figure 5-1

Electricity
Cost Calculator *(cont.)*

Spreadsheets

Activity 5

Procedure

1. Open a new spreadsheet document using Google Docs.

2. At the top of the document in the **Unsaved Spreadsheet** box, type your last name and "Electricity Cost Calculator." Click **OK** in the **Rename Document** window (Figure 5-2).

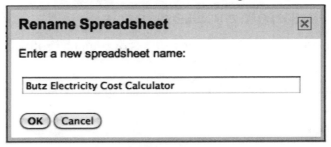

Figure 5-2

3. Spreadsheets are made up of columns that are identified by letters (A, B, C, etc.) and rows that are identified by numbers (1, 2, 3, etc.).

4. The location within a spreadsheet where a column meets a row is called a *cell*, and is identified by both a letter and number (Figure 5-3).

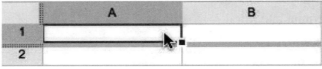

Figure 5-3

5. Click into cell **A1** and enter the following column label: "Appliance."

6. Next, increase its font size to **12 pt** by clicking the **Font size** button (Figure 5-4)

Figure 5-4

7. Now use the **Bold** button (**B**) located just to the right of the **Font Size** button to make the font bold.

8. Now center your label within its cell using the **Align** button (Figure 5-5).

Figure 5-5

9. Hit the **Tab** key on your keyboard to move you over to cell **B1**. Now type the following column heading: "Hours/Day Used." Center the label in its cell, increase its font size to **12 pt**, and also make it **bold**.

Electricity
Cost Calculator *(cont.)*
Activity 5

10. Next, you will have to widen column B so that its label fits on one line. To do this, take your cursor and bring it between columns **B** and **C**, then click and drag to the right until column B is wide enough (Figure 5-6).

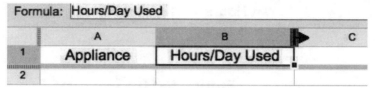

Formula: | Hours/Day Used

	A	B	C
1	Appliance	Hours/Day Used	
2			

Figure 5-6

11. Use Figure 5-7 below to complete setting up your spreadsheet headings. Make sure to increase the font size to **12 pt**, center the text in each cell, and make the text **bold**.

	A	B	C	D	E	F
1	Appliance	Hours/Day Used	Watts	Watt Hours	Kilowatt Hours	Cost of Use
2						

Figure 5-7

12. Next, you are going to change the fill color for your headings. Click and drag over all the cells you created in Row 1 to highlight them, then click on the **Text background color** button and choose **light gray**. (Figure 5-8).

Text background color

Figure 5-8

13. Now click into cell **A2**, and enter "26-inch LCD TV." Hit the **Enter** key on your keyboard to bring you down to cell **A3**. Type "Window Fan."

14. Finally, click into cell **A4** and type "Personal Computer."

15. Next, use the information in Figure 5-9 below to fill in the electrical-use data for each appliance. Make sure to center the text in each cell.

	A	B	C
1	Appliance	Hours/Day Used	Watts
2	26-inch LCD TV	5	110
3	Window Fan	10	150
4	Personal Computer	5	125

Figure 5-9

16. Now click into cell **D2**. In this cell you will insert a formula that will calculate the amount of watt hours used by the television. Watt hours is simply the amount of watts multiplied by the number of hours used for an electrical device. In cell **D2**, type "=B2*C2," then hit the **Enter** key. The = sign tells the cell that there is a formula and to perform the calculation that follows it. The * symbol instructs the formula to multiply. The product of 5 hours x 110 watts, which is 550 watt hours, should now appear in cell **D2**.

Electricity
Cost Calculator *(cont.)*

Activity 5

17. Now you can easily apply the formula to the data in rows 3 and 4. Click back into cell **D2**, and grab the blue anchor point located at the bottom right of the cell (Figure 5-10).

Watt Hours	Kilowatt Hours
550	

Figure 5-10

18. Click and drag to highlight cells **D3** and **D4**. The formula will now automatically be applied, and the products will appear in cells **D3** and **D4** (Figure 5-11).

D	E
Watt Hours	**Kilowatt Hours**
550	
1500	
625	

Figure 5-11

19. Next, click into cell **E2**. In this cell, you will enter the formula to calculate the amount of kilowatt-hours each appliance uses. A kilowatt-hour is equal to 1,000 watt-hours. Enter the following formula in cell **E2**: "=D2/1000." The / symbol instructs the formula to divide. Hit the **Enter** key to apply the formula.

20. Now, click back into cell **E2**, grab the anchor point, and drag down through cells **E3** and **E4** to apply the formula to rows 3 and 4. The quotients will appear in these cells.

21. Next, click into cell **F2**. Here you will enter a formula to determine the cost in dollars and cents of operating each appliance. The national average cost per kilowatt-hour of electricity is 11 cents. In cell **F2**, type the following formula: "=E2*0.11." Hit the **Enter** key on your keyboard to apply the formula to the cell.

22. Now click back into cell **F2**, grab the anchor point, and drag down through cells **F3** and **F4** to apply the formula to rows 3 and 4. The quotients will appear in these cells.

23. Click on column header **F** to select the entire column. You will now change the format of the numbers in this column to display as currency. Go to the **More formats** button and choose the **Currency** option with two decimal places (Figure 5-12).

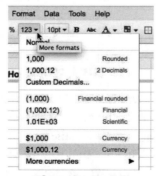

Figure 5-12

Electricity
Cost Calculator (cont.)

Activity 5

24. The cost of electricity of operating each appliance should now display as currency (Figure 5-13). Make sure to center all numbers in all the cells using the **Align** button.

F
Cost of Use
$0.06
$0.17
$0.07

Figure 5-13

25. Next, click into cell **A5** and type "Totals." Make it bold by using the **Bold** button (**B**) and center it within the cell. Hit the **Tab** key to move you into cell **B5**. Now you are going to use the **Functions** tool (Figure 5-14) to insert a function that will total the numbers in each column.

Figure 5-14

26. Click the **Functions** button and select **SUM** (Figure 5-15).

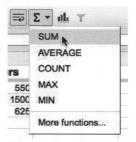

Figure 5-15

27. The SUM function will now be inserted into cell B5. Next, you need to select the cells to add together. To do this, just click and drag over cells B2 through B4 (Figure 5-16).

	A	B
1	**Appliance**	**Hours/Day Used**
2	26-inch LCD TV	5
3	Window Fan	10
4	Personal Computer	5
5	Total	=SUM(B2:B4)
6		

Figure 5-16

28. Next, hit the **Enter** key, and the sum of cells B2 through B4 should appear in cell B5. Click back into cell **B5** and center the number using the **Align** button.

29. Insert the SUM function into cells C5 through F5, and center the numbers.

30. Your project is now complete!

Major Crops of the United States

Activity 6

Objectives

Each student will utilize the Google Docs spreadsheet application to create a column chart showing the amount of the major agricultural crops grown in the United States.

Benchmarks for Technology Standards

Students will know the characteristics, uses, and basic features of computer software programs, including:

- using the common features of spreadsheets
- using spreadsheet software to update, add, and delete data, and to produce charts

Learning Objectives

At the end of this lesson, students will be able to:

1. know the various terms associated with spreadsheets, including rows, columns, and cells
2. enter data into a spreadsheet
3. adjust the width of a selected column
4. change the alignment of data within a cell
5. change the style of data within a cell
6. create and format a column chart from data entered within a spreadsheet

Before the Computer

This activity uses data from the 2000 agricultural census. The number of acres for each crop represents the amount actually harvested. The sales figure is the cash receipt sales for the farmer growing the crops. An example of a completed project is shown in Figure 6-1.

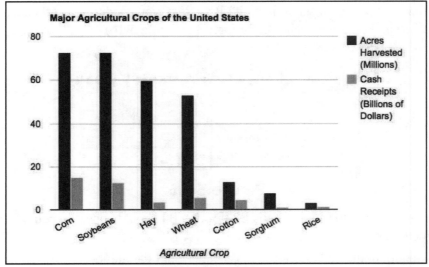

Figure 6-1

Major Crops
of the United States *(cont.)*

Activity 6

Procedure

1. Open a new spreadsheet document using Google Docs.

2. At the top of the document in the **Unsaved spreadsheet** box, type your last name and then "Major Crops of the U. S." Click **OK** in the **Save spreadsheet** window.

3. Spreadsheets are made up of columns that are identified by letters (A, B, C, etc.) and rows that are identified by numbers (1, 2, 3, etc.).

4. The location within a spreadsheet where a column meets a row is called a *cell*, and is identified by both a letter and number (Figure 6-2).

Figure 6-2

5. Click into cell **A1** and type the following label: "Crop."

6. Next, hit the **Tab** key on your keyboard. This will you move you over into cell **B1**. Now type "Acres Harvested (Millions)."

7. Hit the **Tab** key again to move you into cell **C1** and type "Cash Receipts (Billions of Dollars)."

8. Click and drag over cells **A1**, **B1**, and **C1** to highlight them. Use the **Align** button to center the labels in their cells and the **Bold** button (**B**) to make them bold (Figure 6-3).

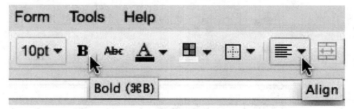

Figure 6-3

9. Now you will have to widen columns B and C so the labels fit on one line within the cell. To do this, take your cursor and bring it to the line between column **B** and **C** at the top of the spreadsheet. Then click and drag to the right until column B is wide enough (Figure 6-4).

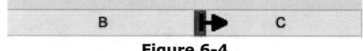

Figure 6-4

10. Repeat the same procedure to widen column C, clicking between columns C and D.

Activity 6

11. Next, use Figure 6-5 below to fill the rest of the data into your spreadsheet.

Crop	Acres Harvested (Millions)	Cash Receipts (Billions of Dollars)
Corn	72.7	15.1
Soybeans	72.7	12.5
Hay	59.9	3.4
Wheat	53.0	5.5
Cotton	13.1	4.6
Sorghum	7.7	.82
Rice	3.0	1.2

Figure 6-5

12. Make sure to center the data in each cell using the **Align** button. You can click and drag over all the cells in columns **A**, **B**, and **C** to highlight them, then use the **Align** button to center them all at once.

13. Next, click into cell **A1** and go to the **Insert** menu and choose **Chart**, or click on the **Insert chart...** button (Figure 6-6).

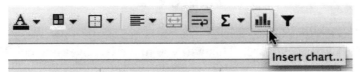

Figure 6-6

14. You will now use the **Chart Editor** window to create a column chart. Make sure there is a check mark in the **Use row 1 as headers** box, then click the **Charts** link (Figure 6-7).

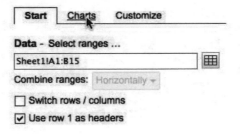

Figure 6-7

15. Next, under **Charts**, click on **Column** and select **column chart**, which is the one above **stacked column chart** (Figure 6-8).

Figure 6-8

16. A preview of your chart will now appear in the Preview window. Now click on the **Customize** link.

Major Crops
of the United States *(cont.)*

Activity 6

17. In the **Customize** window, click in the **Chart Title** box and type "Major Agricultural Crops of the United States" (Figure 6-9). The chart title should now appear above your chart. Hit the **Enter** key or click out of that box.

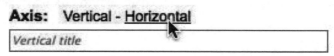

Chart: Title - Name

Major Agricultural Crops of the United States

Figure 6-9

18. Next, click the **Horizontal** axis link. (Figure 6-10).

Axis: Vertical - Horizontal

Vertical title

Figure 6-10

19 In the **Horizontal** axis box, type in the following label: "Agricultural Crop."

20. Next, under **Style**, click the color box and change the column colors for the **Acres Harvested** to **green**.

21. Click the drop-down menu to select the **Cash Receipts** column (Figure 6-11) and change its color to **purple**.

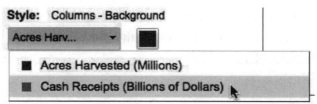

Style: Columns - Background

Acres Harv...

■ Acres Harvested (Millions)

■ Cash Receipts (Billions of Dollars)

Figure 6-11

22. Now that your chart has been set up, click the **Insert** button located at the bottom-right corner of the **Chart Editor** window.

23. Finally, to display your chart as its own page within your spreadsheet, click on the chart, and select the **Chart 1** menu located in the upper-left corner of the chart (Figure 6-12).

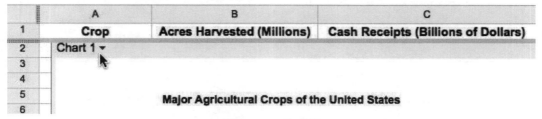

	A	B	C
1	Crop	Acres Harvested (Millions)	Cash Receipts (Billions of Dollars)
2	Chart 1 ▾		
3			
4			
5		Major Agricultural Crops of the United States	
6			

Figure 6-12

24. Under the **Chart 1** menu, select the **Move to own sheet...** option. This will insert your chart on its own page. Your project is now complete!

Climographs

Activity 7

Spreadsheets

Objectives

Each student will utilize the Google Docs spreadsheet application to create a combination line-column chart showing the changes in the mean average temperature and precipitation for Chicago, Illinois.

Benchmarks for Technology Standards

Students will know the characteristics, uses, and basic features of computer software programs, including:

- using the common features of spreadsheets
- using spreadsheet software to update, add, and delete data, and to produce charts

Learning Objectives

At the end of this lesson, students will be able to:

1. know the various terms associated with spreadsheets, including rows, columns, and cells
2. enter data into a spreadsheet
3. adjust the width of a selected column
4. change the alignment of data within a cell
5. change the style of data within a cell
6. use the Autofill function to enter data into a column with a spreadsheet
7. create and format a line-column chart from data entered within a spreadsheet

Before the Computer

This activity is written using the mean average temperature and precipitation for Chicago, Illinois. If you prefer to have your students create a climograph for a different location, visit the following website to get the climate information for any city in the world: **http://www.worldclimate.com**. An example of a completed project is shown in Figure 7-1.

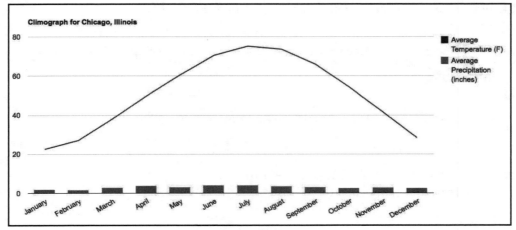

Figure 7-1

Climographs *(cont.)*

Activity 7

Procedure

1. Open a new spreadsheet document using Google Docs.

2. At the top of the document in the **Unsaved spreadsheet** box, type your last name and then "Climograph." Click OK in the Save **Spreadsheet** window.

3. Spreadsheets are made up of columns that are identified by letters (A, B, C, etc.) and rows that are identified by numbers (1, 2, 3, etc.).

4. The location within a spreadsheet where a column meets a row is called a *cell*, and is identified by both a letter and number (Figure 7-2).

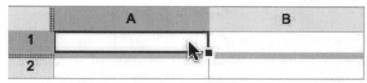

Figure 7-2

5. Click into cell **A1** and type in the following label: "Month."

6. Next, hit the **Tab** key on your keyboard. This will move you over into cell **B1**. Now type "Average Temperature (F)."

7. Hit the **Tab** key again to move into cell **C1** and type "Average Precipitation (inches)."

8. Click and drag over cells **A1**, **B1**, and **C1** to highlight them. Use the **Align** button to center the labels in their cells and the **Bold** button (**B**) to make them bold (Figure 7-3).

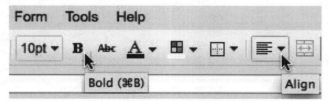

Figure 7-3

9. Now you will have to widen columns **B** and **C** so the labels will fit on one line. To do this, take your cursor and bring it to the line between columns **B** and **C** at the top of the spreadsheet. Then click and drag it to the right until column B is wide enough (Figure 7-4).

Figure 7-4

10. Repeat the same procedure for widening column C, clicking between columns C and D.

11. Next, click into cell **A2** and type "January." Now hit the **Enter** key on your keyboard. This will take you down to cell **A3**. Type in "February."

12. Next, you are going to use the **Autofill** function to automatically fill in the remaining months in column A. Click and drag over cells **A2** and **A3** to highlight them.

Climographs (cont.)

Activity 7

13. With the cells still highlighted, move your cursor to the bottom-right corner of cell **A3** until it changes into a cross (Figure 7-5).

	A	B
1	**Month**	**Average Temperature (F)**
2	January	
3	February	
4		
5		

Figure 7-5

14. Now click and drag down until you get to cell **A13**. Let go of the mouse, and all the months of the year should have automatically been inserted into your spreadsheet.

15. Next, enter the data on the temperature and precipitation for each month using the data in Figure 7-6.

Month	Average Temperature (F)	Average Precipitation (inches)
January	22.5	1.9
February	27	1.6
March	38	2.8
April	49.6	3.8
May	60.4	3.2
June	70.3	4.1
July	75	4
August	73.4	3.5
September	65.8	3.1
October	54.1	2.7
November	41.4	2.9
December	28.2	2.6

Figure 7-6

16. Once your data is entered, click and drag over columns **A**, **B**, and **C** to highlight them and use the **Align** button to center the data in the cells.

17. Next, click into cell **A1**, go to the **Insert** menu, and choose **Chart**, or click on the **Insert chart…** button (Figure 7-7).

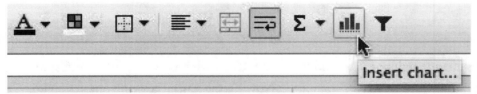

Figure 7-7

Spreadsheets

18. You will now use the **Chart Editor** window to create a line-column chart. Make sure there is a check mark in the **Use row 1 as headers** box, then click the **Charts** link (Figure 7-8).

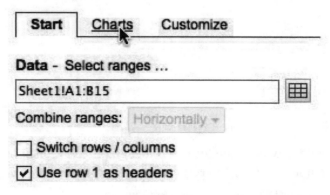

Figure 7-8

19. Next, under **Charts**, click on **Line** and select the **combo chart** (Figure 7-9).

Figure 7-9

20. A preview of your chart will now appear in the **Preview** window. Now click on the **Customize** link.

21. In the **Customize** window, click in the **Chart Title** box and type "Climograph for Chicago, Illinois." The chart title should now appear above your chart (Figure 7-10).

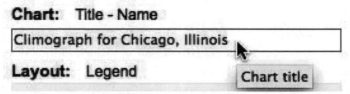

Figure 7-10

22. Next, you are going to make the temperature data appear as a line on your chart and the precipitation data as columns, which is standard for a climograph.

Climographs (cont.)

Activity 7

23. Under **Data Series**, click the drop-down menu next to **Type** and change it to **Line** (Figure 7-11).

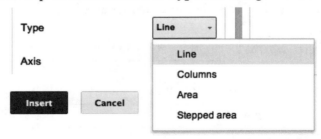

Figure 7-11

24. The temperature data should now be in the form of a line graph. Now click on the **Average Temperature** drop-down box, and switch it to **Average Precipitation** (Figure 7-12).

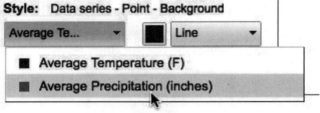

Figure 7-12

25. Change the **Precipitation** data to show on the graph as **Columns** (Figure 7-13).

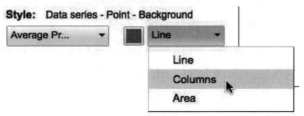

Figure 7-13

26. Now that your chart has been set-up, click the **Insert** button located at the bottom-right corner of the **Chart Editor** window.

27. Finally, to display your chart as its own page within your spreadsheet, click on the chart, and select the **Chart 1** menu located in the upper left-corner of the chart (Figure 7-14).

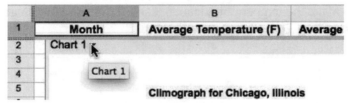

Figure 7-14

28. Under the **Chart 1** menu, select the **Move to own sheet…** option. This will insert your chart on its own page. Your project is now complete!

What's in Seawater?

Activity 8

Objectives

Each student will utilize the Google Docs spreadsheet application to create a pie chart showing the composition of seawater.

Benchmarks for Technology Standards

Students will know the characteristics, uses, and basic features of computer software programs, including:

- using the common features of spreadsheets
- using spreadsheet software to update, add, and delete data, and to produce charts

Learning Objectives

At the end of this lesson, students will be able to:

1. know the various terms associated with spreadsheets, including rows, columns, and cells
2. enter data into a spreadsheet
3. change the alignment of data within a cell
4. change the style of data within a cell
5. change the format of numbers to display as percentages
6. change the color of a cell
7. add a border around a cell
8. create and format a pie chart from data entered within a spreadsheet

Variations

This activity is written using the major components of seawater expressed as a percentage, but any data that is in the form of a percentage out of 100 can be substituted to better fit your curriculum. Just make sure you enter your data in the form of a decimal if you plan to alter this activity. An example of a completed project is shown in Figure 8-1.

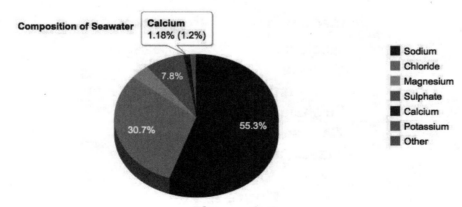

Figure 8-1

What's in Seawater? *(cont.)*

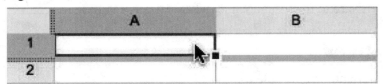

Activity 8

Procedure

1. Open a new spreadsheet document using Google Docs.

2. At the top of the document in the **Unsaved spreadsheet** box, type your last name and "Seawater." Click **OK** in the **Save Spreadsheet** window.

3. Spreadsheets are made up of columns that are identified by letters (A, B, C, etc.) and rows that are identified by numbers (1, 2, 3, etc.).

4. The location within a spreadsheet where a column meets a row is called a *cell*, and is identified by both a letter and number (Figure 8-2).

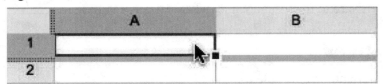

Figure 8-2

5. Click into cell **A1** and type in the following label: "Element or Ion."

6. Next, hit the **Tab** key on your keyboard. This will move you over into cell **B1**. Now type "Percentage."

7. Click and drag over cells **A1** and **B1** to highlight them. Use the **Align** button to center the labels in their cells and the **Bold** button (**B**) to make them bold (Figure 8-3).

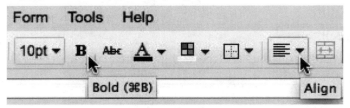

Figure 8-3

8. Next, click into cell **A2** and type "Sodium." Now hit the **Tab** key on your keyboard. This will take you over to cell **B2**. Type "0.5529."

9. Use the following table to complete entering your data.

Element or Ion	Percentage
Sodium	0.5529
Chloride	0.3074
Magnesium	0.0369
Sulphate	0.0775
Calcium	0.0118
Potassium	0.0114
Other	0.0021

Figure 8-4

What's in Seawater? *(cont.)*

Activity 8

10. Once your data is entered, click and drag over both columns **A** and **B** to highlight them, and use the **Align** button to center the data in the cells.

11. Now you will change the format of the numbers in column **B** so they display as percentages. Highlight the numbers by clicking and dragging over them.

12. Next, click the **Format as percent** button (Figure 8-5).

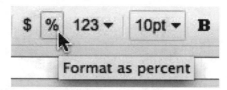

Figure 8-5

13. Now you are going to change the background color of the cells within your spreadsheet. Click and drag over all of your data to highlight it, then click the **Text background color** button (Figure 8-6). Select a light blue color.

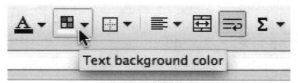

Figure 8-6

14. Next, with your data still highlighted, you will add a border around the cells. Click the **Borders** button and choose the option for inside and outside borders (Figure 8-7).

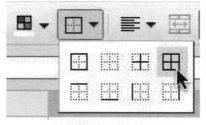

Figure 8-7

15. Now, you are going to display your data in the form of a pie chart. Click into cell **A1**, then go to the **Insert** menu and choose **Chart**, or click on the **Insert Chart...** button (Figure 8-8).

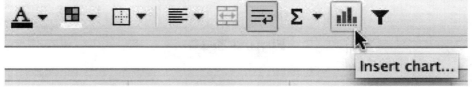

Figure 8-8

16. You will now use the **Chart Editor** window to create a pie chart. Make sure there is a check mark in the **Use row 1 as headers** box.

17. Next, under the **Charts** link, click on **Pie** and select **3d pie chart**, which is the option below **pie chart** (Figure 8-9).

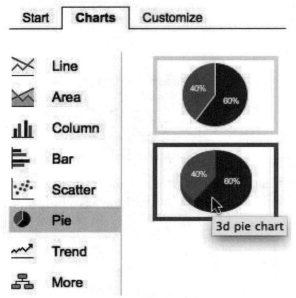

Figure 8-9

18. A preview of your chart will now appear in the **Preview** window. Now click on the **Customize** link.

19. In the **Customize** window, click in the **Chart Title** box and type "Composition of Seawater." Then click out of that box. The chart title should now appear above your chart.

20. Next, under the **Style** menu, you can select a specific series of data and change the color of its pie slice within the chart. For example, click on the drop-down menu and select **Chloride** (Figure 8-10).

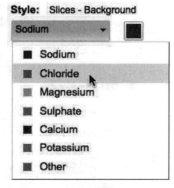

Figure 8-10

What's in Seawater? *(cont.)*

Activity 8

21. Change the color of chloride's pie slice to gray by clicking on the color box and selecting the color **gray** (Figure 8-11).

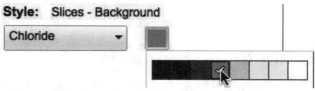

Figure 8-11

22. Now that your chart has been set up, click the **Insert** button located at the bottom-right corner of the **Chart Editor** window.

23. Finally, to display your chart as its own page within your spreadsheet, click on the chart and select the **Chart 1** menu located in the upper-left corner.

24. Under the **Chart 1** menu, select the **Move to own sheet...** option. This will insert your chart on its own page (Figure 8-12).

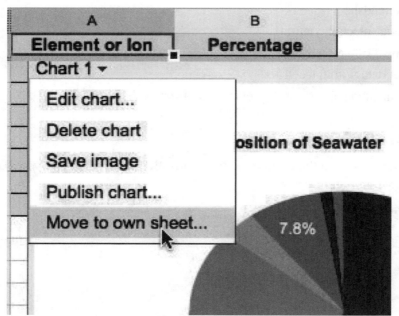

Figure 8-12

25. Try hovering over a pie slice with your cursor. That should produce a pop-up of the data for each pie slice. Your project is now complete!

Human Population Growth

Activity 9

Objectives

Each student will utilize the Google Docs spreadsheet application to create an area chart showing the changes in world human population.

Benchmarks for Technology Standards

Students will know the characteristics, uses, and basic features of computer software programs, including:

- using the common features and of spreadsheets
- using spreadsheet software to update, add, and delete data, and to produce charts

Learning Objectives

At the end of this lesson, students will be able to:

1. know the various terms associated with spreadsheets, including rows, columns, and cells
2. enter data into a spreadsheet
3. adjust the width of a selected column
4. change the alignment of data within a cell
5. change the style of data within a cell
6. create and format an area chart from data entered in a spreadsheet

Before the Computer

For the current population data, visit the Population Reference Bureau at **http://www.prb.org**. An example of a completed project is shown in Figure 9-1.

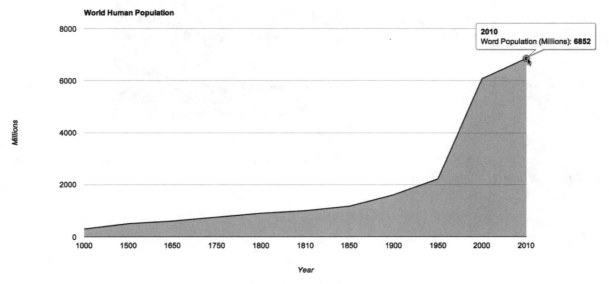

Figure 9-1

Human Population Growth *(cont.)*

Spreadsheets

Activity 9

Procedure

1. Open a new spreadsheet document using Google Docs.

2. At the top of the document in the **Unsaved spreadsheet** box, type your last name and "Human Population." Click **OK** in the **Save spreadsheet** window.

3. Spreadsheets are made up of columns that are identified by letters (A, B, C, etc.) and rows that are identified by numbers (1, 2, 3, etc.).

4. The location within a spreadsheet where a column meets a row is called a *cell*, and is identified by both a letter and number (Figure 9-2).

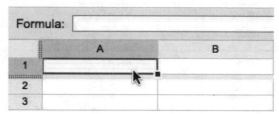

Figure 9-2

5. Click into cell **A1** and enter the following column label: "Year."

6. Hit the **Tab** key on your keyboard to move you over to cell **B1** and type "World Population (Millions)."

7. Next, highlight all of the labels in row 1 by clicking and dragging over them, increase their font size to **12 pt** by clicking the **Font size** button, and use the **Bold** button (**B**) to make the font bold (Figure 9-3).

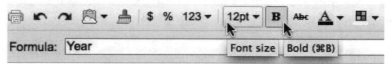

Figure 9-3

8. Now center your labels by using the **Align** button (Figure 9-4).

Figure 9-4

9. Now you will widen column B so that its label fits on one line. Move your cursor to the line between columns B and C. Then click and drag toward the right until column B is wide enough (Figure 9-5).

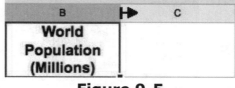

Figure 9-5

Human Population Growth *(cont.)*

Activity 9

10. Next, use the data below to fill out the rest of your spreadsheet.

Year	World Population (millions)
1000	300
1500	500
1650	600
1750	750
1800	900
1810	1000
1850	1171
1900	1608
1950	2216
2000	6080
2010	6852

11. Once your data is entered, highlight it by clicking and dragging over it, then center it using the **Align** button.

12. With your data still highlighted, change the font size to **12** using the **Font Size** button.

13. Next, you are going to use your data to make an area chart. Click into cell **A1**, then go to the **Insert** menu and choose **Chart**, or you can click the **Insert chart...** button (Figure 9-6).

Figure 9-6

14. You will now use the **Chart Editor** window to create a line chart. Make sure there is a check mark in the **Use row 1 as headers** box, then put a check mark in the **Use column A as labels** box. Now click the **Charts** link.

15. Next, under **Charts**, click on **Area** and select **area chart**, which is the one above **stacked area chart** (Figure 9-7).

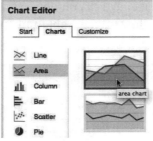

Figure 9-7

Human Population Growth (cont.)

Activity 9

16. A preview of your chart will now appear in the **Preview** window. Next click on the **Customize** link.

17. In the **Customize** window, click in the **Chart Title** box and type "World Human Population." Then click out of that box. The chart title should now appear above your chart.

18. Next, under **Legend**, click **None** (Figure 9-8).

Figure 9-8

20. Now click into the **Axis: Vertical** box and type in the name of your vertical axis, which is "Millions." Next, click the **Horizontal** axis link.

21. In the **Axis: Horizontal** box, type in the following label: "Year." Then click out of that box.

22. Now that your chart is set up, click the **Insert** button located at the bottom-right corner of the **Chart Editor** window.

23. Finally, to display your chart as its own page within your spreadsheet, click on the chart, and select the menu located in the upper-right corner of the chart.

24. Under the drop-down menu, select the **Move to own sheet...** option. This will insert your chart on its own page. Your project is now complete!

National Weather Map

Activity 10

Objectives

Each student will utilize the Google Docs drawing application to create a map using common weather map symbols that show the current state of the weather in the United States.

Benchmarks for Technology Standards

Students will know the characteristics, uses, and basic features of computer software programs, including:

- using the common features of desktop publishing and word processing software
- knowing that documents can be created, designed, and formatted

Learning Objectives

At the end of this lesson, students will be able to:

1. insert an image into a drawing document
2. use the line tool
3. use the polygon tool
4. change the fill and line color of a shape
5. change the thickness and color of a line
6. use the text box tool
7. change the size, color, and style of font within a text box
8. rotate and resize objects in a drawing
9. copy and paste an object in a drawing

Before the Computer

This activity requires the use of a map image of the United States, which needs to be saved in a location for students to access. You can download a free version from the following website, **http://www.worldatlas.com/webimage/countrys/namerica/usstates/usashape.htm**. Save this file in a shared class folder before beginning this lesson. You may also wish to instruct your students to go to the above website and save the image on their computers before beginning the activity. An example of a completed project is shown in Figure 10-1.

Drawing

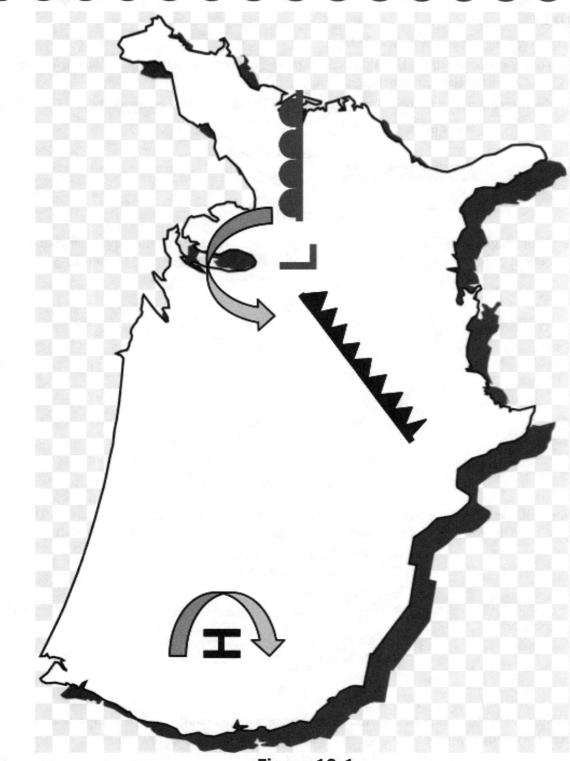

Figure 10-1

National
Weather Map *(cont.)*

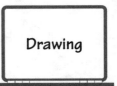

Activity 10

Procedure

1. Open a new drawing document in Google Docs.

2. At the top of the document in the **Untitled drawing** box, type your last name and "National Weather Map." Click **OK** in the **Rename Document** window.

3. Click on the **Insert** menu and choose **Image**. Click on **Upload**, then hit the **Browse** button (Figure 10-2).

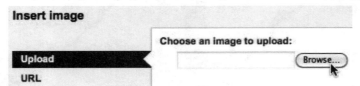

Figure 10-2

4. Navigate to the map file on your computer. Click **Open**. The image should now appear in your drawing. Grab the bottom-right anchor point and enlarge the map so that it fills your page (Figure 10-3).

Figure 10-3

5. Next, you will open a new window in your web browser so you can view the latest national weather map. To do this, go to the **File** menu of your web browser and choose **New Window** (Figure 10-4).

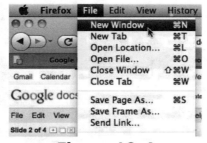

Figure 10-4

6. Next, navigate to the following web address: **http://www.weather.com**. Click the **Maps** menu and choose **US Current Weather**. Most national weather maps show the locations of low- and high-atmospheric pressure along with the location of cold and warm fronts. Use this webpage as a guide to creating your weather map.

National Weather Map *(cont.)*

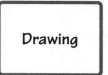
Drawing

Activity 10

7. First, you will add the locations of the low- and high-pressure symbols. Low pressure is noted on a weather map as a red L and high pressure a blue H. Return to your Google Docs drawing window and click the **Text box** button (Figure 10-5).

Figure 10-5

8. Click and drag the text box tool to draw a square in the low-pressure location (Figure 10-6).

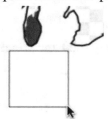

Figure 10-6

9. In the text box, type an uppercase "L," then hit **Enter** on your keyboard.

10. Next, click on the **Font size** button and increase the size of your L to **48 pt** (Figure 10-7).

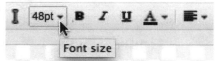

Figure 10-7

11. Now use the **Bold** button to make the L bold, and change its color to red using the **Text color** button (Figure 10-8).

Figure 10-8

12. Next you are going to draw in the location of a cold front, which is usually associated with the low-pressure location. A cold front symbol is a blue line with triangles pointing in the direction the front is moving. First, click on the **Line** tool (Figure 10-9). If you don't see the Line tool in your toolbar, go to the **Insert** menu and select the **Line** tool.

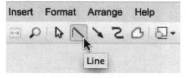

Figure 10-9

Drawing

Activity 10

13. Use the line tool to draw a line showing the location of the cold front (Figure 10-10).

Figure 10-10

14. Next, increase the line thickness to **8** using the **Line weight** button (Figure 10-11).

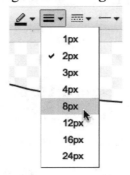

Figure 10-11

15. Also change the line color to **blue** using the **Line color** button (Figure 10-12).

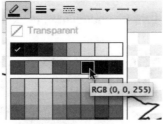

Figure 10-12

16. Next, you will use the **Polyline** tool (Figure 10-13) to draw the triangles on the cold front line. The **Polyline** tool allows you draw an irregular shaped object. Every time you click as you draw, the line continues until you double-click to end it. If you don't see the Polyline tool in your toolbar, go to the **Insert** menu, choose **Line**, and select the **Polyline** tool.

Figure 10-13

Activity 10

17. Select the **Polyline** tool and click it on the end of the blue line. Move your cursor out, click once to create an anchor point, then move your cursor back toward the blue line to make a triangle (Figure 10-14).

Figure 10-14

18. Now continue to use your **Polyline** tool to make a series of triangles along the blue line (Figure 10-15).

Figure 10-15

19. When you get to the end of the blue line, double-click and your polygon will be completed (Figure 10-16).

Figure 10-16

20. Next, you will use the **Fill color** tool to change the color of the polygon's fill to the same blue as the blue line. Click the **Fill color** button and select **blue** (Figure 10-17).

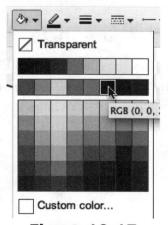

Figure 10-17

Drawing

21. Now click on the **Line** tool again and use it to draw a line out from the low-pressure symbol (Figure 10-18).

Figure 10-18

22. Next, use the **Line color** button and change the color of the line to **red**. Also increase its width to **8 pt**. This line will represent a warm front, which is drawn as a red line with red semicircles pointing in the direction the front is moving.

23. Now you will use the **Shapes** tool to draw a semi-circle to add to the warm front line. Click on **Shape**, choose **Shapes**, and select the **Chord** shape (Figure 10-19).

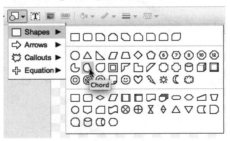

Figure 10-19

24. Use the **Shape** tool to draw a small semi-circle (Figure 10-20).

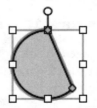

Figure 10-20

25. Change the line and fill colors to **red** using the **Line color** and **Fill color** buttons.

26. Now grab the anchor point at the top of the semi-circle, drag it to the right, and rotate the shape about 90 degrees so the circle is pointing up (Figure 10-21). You may need to click and drag the lower-right anchor point to decrease its size as well.

Figure 10-21

Activity 10

27. Next, click and drag the circle over to the red line, and place it just on top of the line (Figure 10-22).

Figure 10-22

28. With the circle still highlighted, go to the **Edit** menu, choose **Copy**, then **Paste**. A copy of the circle will appear next to the first one you drew. Click and drag it onto the red line next to the first circle. Choose **Paste** again to create another copy. Continue to paste circles until the warm front symbol is complete (Figure 10-23).

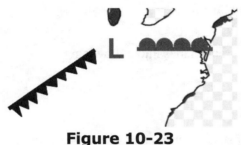

Figure 10-23

29. Next, Use the **Text box** tool to create a high-pressure symbol "H" and place it in the correct location. Make it **bold**, change its color to **blue**, and increase its font size to **48 pt**.

30. Sometimes weather maps show the movement of winds associated with pressure centers. In the Northern Hemisphere, winds travel in a clockwise direction around high pressure. Click on **Shape**, choose **Arrows**, and select the **Curved Left Arrow** shape (Figure 10-24).

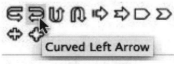

Figure 10-24

31. Now use the **Curved Left Arrow** shape to draw the movement of winds around the high-pressure symbol (Figure 10-25). If you have time, add a Curved Right Arrow shape around the low-pressure symbol. Your project is now complete!

Figure 10-25

Technological Systems Diagram

Drawing

Activity 11

Objectives

Each student will utilize the Google Docs drawing application to create a technological systems diagram for a modern home heating system.

Benchmarks for Technology Standards

Students will know the characteristics, uses, and basic features of computer software programs, including:

- using the common features of desktop publishing and word processing software
- knowing that documents can be created, designed, and formatted

Learning Objectives

At the end of this lesson, students will be able to:

1. insert an image into a drawing document
2. use the Shape tool to insert different shapes into a drawing
3. resize shapes within a drawing
4. flip shapes horizontally and vertically
5. rotate shapes within a drawing
6. change the line and fill color of shapes within a drawing
7. label a shape using the text box tool
8. use the Arrow tool
9. change the size and style of font within a text box
10. insert Word Art into a drawing

Before the Computer

This activity uses a technological systems diagram for a home heating system; however, any technological system can be substituted if it better fits your curriculum. The same basic steps can be followed to create a customized diagram. An example of a completed project is shown in Figure 11-1.

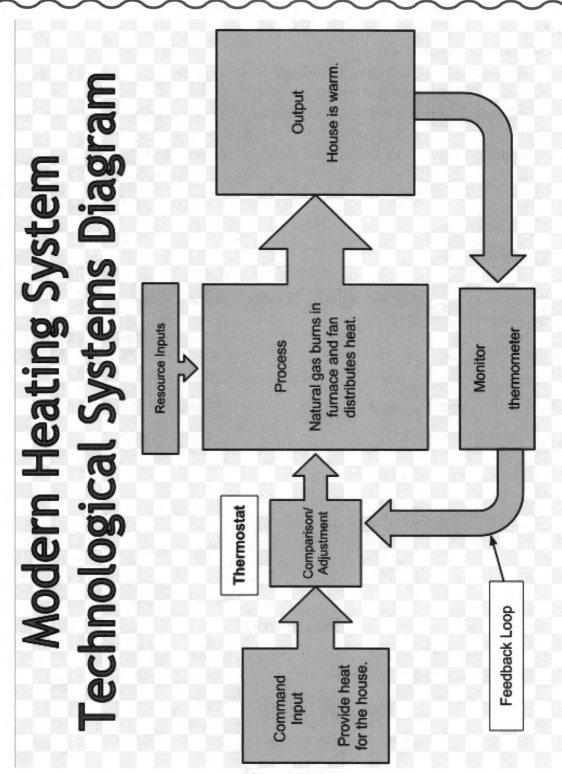

Modern Heating System
Technological Systems Diagram

Output — House is warm.

Resource Inputs

Process — Natural gas burns in furnace and fan distributes heat.

Monitor — thermometer

Thermostat

Comparison/ Adjustment

Command Input — Provide heat for the house.

Feedback Loop

Figure 11-1

Technological Systems Diagram *(cont.)*

Drawing

Activity 11

Procedure

1. Open a new drawing document in Google Docs.

2. At the top of the document in the **Untitled drawing** box, type your last name and "Tech Systems Diagram." Click **OK** in the **Rename Document** window.

3. A technical systems diagram is a flow chart that illustrates all of the basic parts of a technical process. For this activity you will create one that describes a modern home heating system.

4. Click the **Shape** tool, select **Arrows**, and choose the **Right Arrow Callout** shape (Figure 11-2).

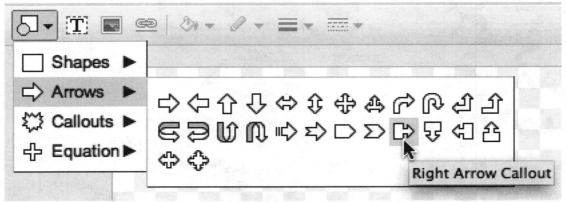

Figure 11-2

5. Click and drag your cursor to draw a rectangle near the middle of the page along the left margin (Figure 11-3).

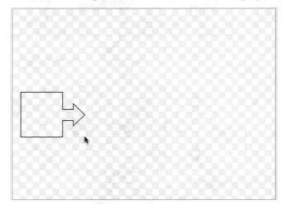

Figure 11-3

6. With the callout shape still highlighted, change its line color to **black** and its fill color to **gray** using the **Line color** and **Fill color** buttons (Figure 11-4).

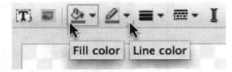

Figure 11-4

7. Next, you will use the **Text box** tool (Figure 11-5) to create a label within the callout shape.

Figure 11-5

8. Select the **Text box** tool and click and drag it to draw a small rectangle in the top-half of the callout shape (Figure 11-6).

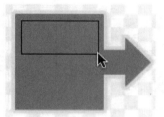

Figure 11-6

9. In the text box, type "Command Input," then hit the **Enter** key on your keyboard to insert your text.

10. Use the **Bold** button to make the text bold within the text box. You may need to adjust the size of the text box to make it fit properly.

11. Select the **Text box** tool again and draw another rectangle in the callout shape right below the text box you just created (Figure 11-7).

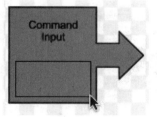

Figure 11-7

12. In the text box, type "Provide heat for the house." Hit **Enter** to insert your text.

13. Next, select **Shape** again, choose **Arrows**, and draw another, smaller **Right Arrow Callout** shape to the right of the first one (Figure 11-8).

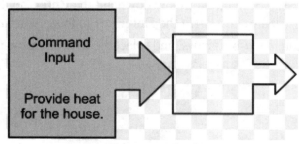

Figure 11-8

14. Double-click on the callout shape to bring up a text box. In the text box, type "Comparison/Adjustment," then hit **Enter** to insert your text. Also change the line color to **black** and the fill color to **gray**.

15. Use the **Font size** button to reduce the size of the text in the callout shape to **12**. If the text does not fit well within the shape, click and drag the lower-right anchor point to increase the shape's size so the text fits within the box.

16. Select the **Text box** tool again and use it to draw a small rectangle directly above the callout shape (Figure 11-9).

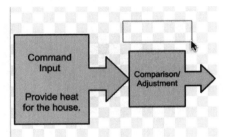

Figure 11-9

17. In the text box, type "Thermostat," then hit **Enter** to insert your text. Use the **Bold** button (**B**) to make the text bold. Also, change the line color of the text box to **black** and the fill to **white** this time.

18. Select the **Shape** button again, and draw a third, larger right arrow callout shape to the right of the second one (Figure 11-10).

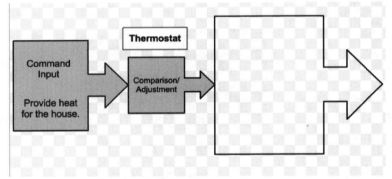

Figure 11-10

19. Change the fill color to **gray** and the line color to **black**. Then double-click the callout shape to bring up a text box, and type "Process." Hold the **Shift** key down, hit the **Enter** key twice, then type "Natural gas burns in furnace and fan distributes heat." Hit the **Enter** key to insert your text.

20. Now select the **Shape** button, choose **Arrows**, and select the **Down Arrow Callout** shape (Figure 11-11).

Figure 11-11

Technological Systems Diagram *(cont.)*

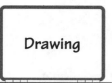

Drawing

Activity 11

21. Click and drag your cursor above the **Process** box you just drew, and draw a small down arrow callout (Figure 11-12).

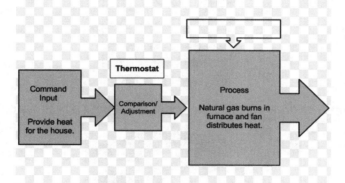

Figure 11-12

22. Change the fill color to **gray** and the line color to **black**, then double-click on the callout box. Enter the following in the text box: "Resource Inputs." Hit **Enter**, then reduce the font size to **12 pt**.

23. Next, select the **Shape** button, choose **Shapes**, and select the **Rectangle** tool (Figure 11-13).

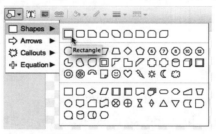

Figure 11-13

24. Use the rectangle tool to draw a large rectangle to the right of the Process box (Figure 11-14).

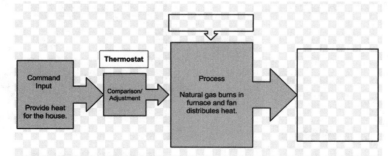

Figure 11-14

25. Double-click in the rectangle to bring up a text box, and type "Output." Hold the **Shift** key down, hit the **Enter** key twice, then type "House is warm." Hit the **Enter** key to insert your text.

26. Change the line color to **black** and the fill to **gray** for the rectangle.

Technological Systems Diagram *(cont.)*

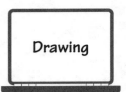

Activity 11

27. Next, select the **Shape** button, choose **Arrows**, and select the **Bent Arrow** shape (Figure 11-15).

Figure 11-15

28. Click and drag your cursor to draw a bent arrow below the Output box (Figure 11-16).

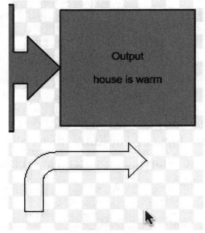

Figure 11-16

29. Change the arrow's line color to **black** and its fill color to **gray**.

30. The arrow is pointing in the wrong direction, so it has to be flipped both vertically and horizontally. Go to the **Arrange** menu, choose **Rotate**, and then select **Flip horizontally** (Figure 11-17).

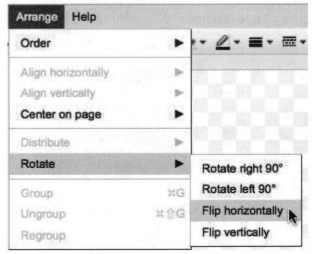

Figure 11-17

31. The arrow should now be pointing toward the left. Return to the **Arrange** menu, choose **Rotate**, and select **Flip vertically**. The arrow should now be in the correct alignment. Click on the **Select** tool (Figure 11-18), then click and drag the arrow so it appears as shown in Figure 11-19.

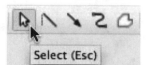

Figure 11-18

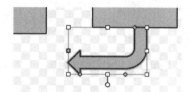

Figure 11-19

32. Now use the **Rectangle** tool again to draw a rectangle below the Process box (Figure 11-20).

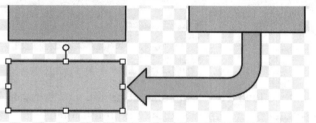

Figure 11-20

33. Double-click in the rectangle to bring up a text box, and type "Monitor," then hold the **Shift** key down, hit the **Enter** key twice, then type "thermometer." Hit the **Enter** key to insert your text. Change the fill color to **gray** and the line color to **black**.

34. Choose the **Bent Arrow** shape again and use it to draw an arrow below the Comparison/Adjustment box (Figure 11-21).

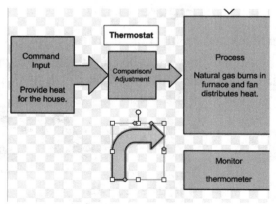

Figure 11-21

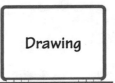
35. Click the anchor point at the top of the arrow and drag the arrow to the left to rotate it 90 degrees (Figure 11-22).

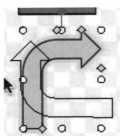

Figure 11-22

36. Now choose the **Select** tool and use it to click and drag the arrow so its end connects to the Monitor box (Figure 11-23).

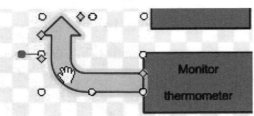

Figure 11-23

37. Next, you will need to extend the arrow so it connects to the Comparison/Adjustment box. Click on the anchor point at the top-center of the arrow and drag it until it touches the box (Figure 11-24).

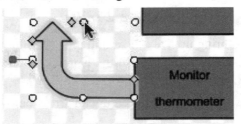

Figure 11-24

38. Now change the line color to **black** and the fill color to **gray**.

39. Next, you will use the **Text box** tool to draw a text box just to the left of the curved arrow. In the text box, type "Feedback Loop." Then change its line color to **black** and its fill color to **white** (Figure 11-25).

Figure 11-25

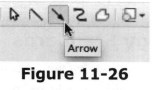
40. Now you will use the **Arrow** tool (Figure 11-26) to draw an arrow from the **Feedback Loop** box to the curved arrow (Figure 11-27). If you don't see the Arrow tool in your tool bar, go to the **Insert** menu and select **Arrow**.

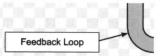

Figure 11-26

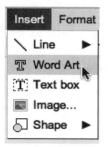

Figure 11-27

41. Your technological systems diagram is complete. Now you will use Word Art to label it. Click on the **Insert** menu and choose **Word Art** (Figure 11-28).

Figure 11-28

42. In the **Word Art** text box, type "Modern Heating System," then hold down the **Shift** key and hit **Enter**. Type "Technological Systems Diagram." Hit the **Enter** key again to insert your text.

43. Click and drag the **Word Art** box to the top-center of your page (Figure 11-29).

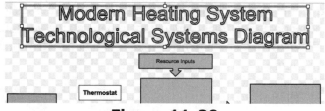

Figure 11-29

44. Now you can change the fill and line color of your Word Art just like you do for shapes in a drawing. You can also change the font by using the **Font** drop-down menu (Figure 11-30).

Figure 11-30

45. Your project is now complete!

Favorite Book, Movie, and TV Show Survey

Activity 12

Objectives

Each student will utilize the Google Docs form application to create a simple survey to gather information about his or her classmates' favorite books, movies, and TV shows. Each student will then analyze his or her results.

Benchmarks for Technology Standards

Students will know the characteristics, uses, and basic features of computer software programs, including:

- using the common features of desktop publishing and word processing software
- knowing that documents can be created, designed, and formatted

Learning Objectives

At the end of this lesson, students will be able to:

1. create a new form

2. add a title and instructions to a form

3. insert a text question into a form

4. format a text question within a form

5. format a check-box question within a form

6. format a multiple-choice question in a form

7. format a grid question in a form

8. email a form to a group

9. view the results of a form

Before the Computer

The use of forms in Google Docs requires students to email one another to get responses. Before beginning this activity, you should prepare a document with all of your students' email addresses to share with the class. It is best to provide them with an online document that contains the emails so they can just copy and paste the email addresses when needed. This alleviates any spelling error mistakes that can disrupt the process. An example form for this activity is shown in Figure 12-1.

Favorite Book, Movie, and TV Show Survey *(cont.)*

Forms

Activity 12

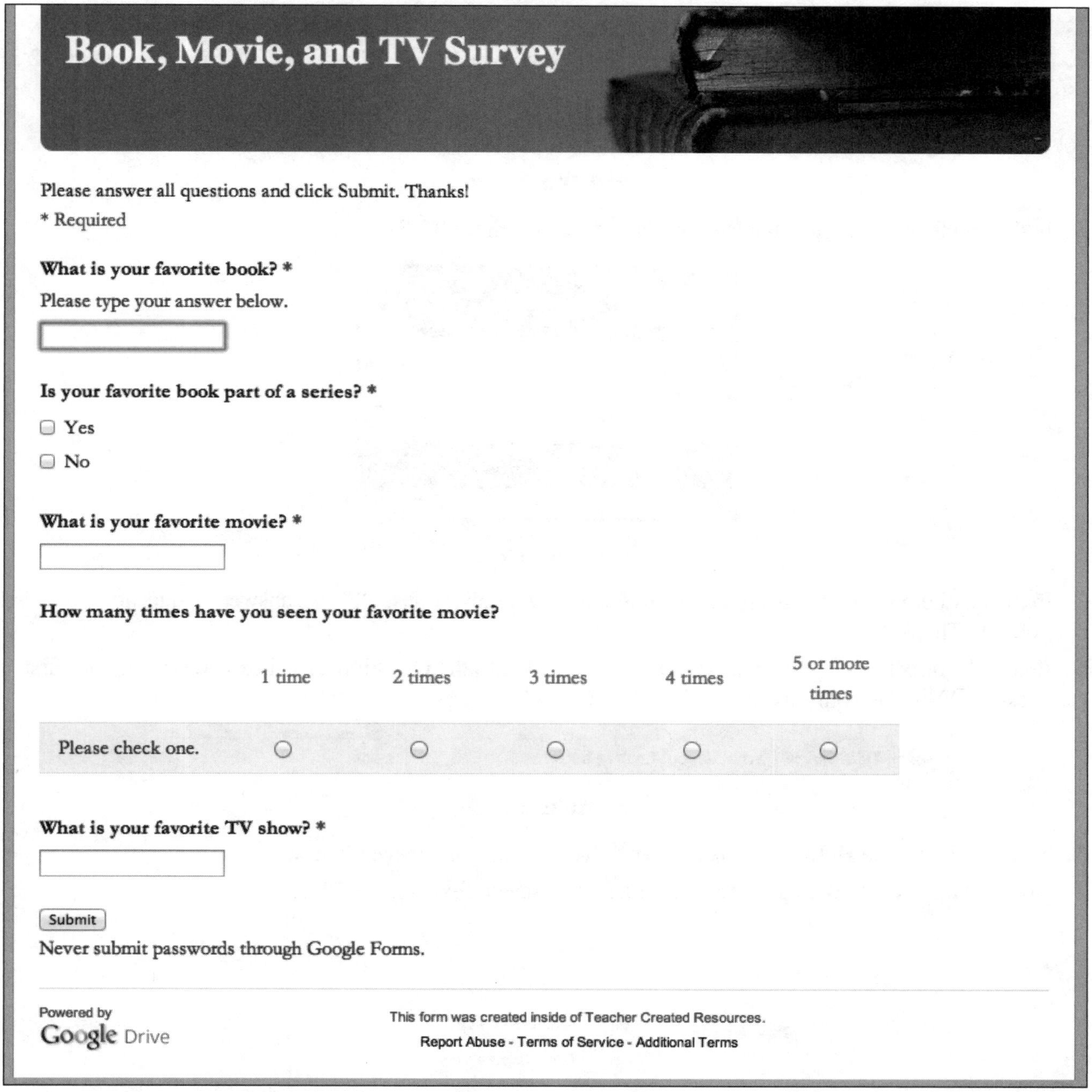

Book, Movie, and TV Survey

Please answer all questions and click Submit. Thanks!

* Required

What is your favorite book? *

Please type your answer below.

Is your favorite book part of a series? *

- Yes
- No

What is your favorite movie? *

How many times have you seen your favorite movie?

	1 time	2 times	3 times	4 times	5 or more times
Please check one.	○	○	○	○	○

What is your favorite TV show? *

Submit

Never submit passwords through Google Forms.

Powered by Google Drive

This form was created inside of Teacher Created Resources.

Report Abuse - Terms of Service - Additional Terms

Figure 12-1

Favorite Book, Movie, and TV Show Survey (cont.)

Forms

Activity 12

Procedure

1. Open a new form document in Google Docs.
2. At the top of the document in the **Untitled Form** box, type "Book, Movie, and TV Survey" (Figure 12-2).

Book, Movie, and TV Survey

Figure 12-2

3. In the theme gallery, select the **Books Classic** theme (Figure 12-3).

Figure 12-3

4. In the box below your form's title, type in the following directions: "Please answer all questions and click Submit. Thanks!"
5. Below the directions box is your first question. Click into the **Question Title** box and type in your first question, "What is your favorite book?" (Figure 12-4).

Question Title	What is your favorite book?

Figure 12-4

6. Next, click into the **Help Text** box and type "Please type your answer below."
7. Now use the **Question Type** drop-down menu and select **Text** (Figure 12-5).

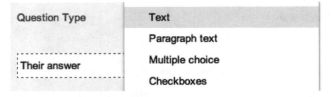

Figure 12-5

8. Put a check mark in the box next to **Required question** and click **Done**.
9. Click **add item** to add another question.
10. Click into the **Question Title** box and type in your next question, "Is your favorite book part of a series?"

Favorite Book, Movie, and TV Show Survey (cont.)

Activity 12

11. Now use the **Question Type** drop-down menu and select **Checkboxes**.

12. Click into the **Option 1** box and type, "Yes." Then click into the **Click to add option** box and type "No" (Figure 12-6).

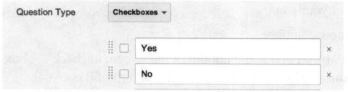

Figure 12-6

13. Put a check mark in the box next to **Required question**, then click **Done**.

14. Next, click on the **Add Item** button located at the upper left-hand side of your page and select **Text** from the drop-down menu (Figure 12-7).

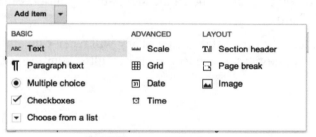

Figure 12-7

15. Now type in your next question in the **Question Title** box: "What is your favorite movie?"

16. Put a check mark in the box next to **Required question**, then click **Done**.

17. Click the **Add Item** button and select a **Grid** question.

18. In the **Question Title** box, type "How many times have you seen your favorite movie?"

19. Now click into the Row 1 label box and type "Please Check One."

20. Next, click into the **Column 1 label** box and type "1 time."

21. Use Figure 12-8 to complete your grid question set-up. Then click **Done**.

Figure 12-8

Favorite Book, Movie, and TV Show Survey *(cont.)*

Activity 12

22. Finally, use the **Add Item** button to insert one more **Text** question.

23. In the **Question Title** box, type "What is your favorite TV show?"

24. Put a check mark in the **Required question** box, then click **Done**. Now click the **Save** button near the upper right-hand side of your page.

25. Your questionnaire is now complete.

26. In the **Confirmation Page** section at the bottom of the screen, uncheck the box next to **Show link to submit another response**. This is the screen that people who fill out your survey will see after they click **Submit**.

27. Your survey is now complete and ready to be used.

28. Next, you will make a list of email contacts to whom you will send your questionnaire. Click on the **Send form** button at the top of your form.

29. In the **Send this via email** window, enter the email addresses of your classmates that were provided by your teacher. Then click **Send**.

30. Your form will now be emailed to your classmates. They will receive an email with a link to the form. You can click on the **View responses** button to view the results. Your project is now complete!

Popular
Sports Survey

Activity 13

Objectives

Each student will utilize the Google Docs form application to create a survey about his or her classmates' favorite sports. He or she will then analyze the results.

Benchmarks for Technology Standards

Students will know the characteristics, uses, and basic features of computer software programs, including:

- using the common features of desktop publishing and word processing software
- knowing that documents can be created, designed, and formatted

Learning Objectives

At the end of this lesson, students will be able to:

1. create a new form
2. add a title and instructions to a form
3. insert a text question into a form
4. format a text question within a form
5. format a choose from list question within a form
6. format a scale question within a form
7. format a multiple-choice question
8. format a checkboxes question in a form
9. change the theme of a form
10. email a form to a group
11. view the results of your form

Before the Computer

The use of forms in Google Docs requires students to email one another to get responses. Before beginning this activity, you should prepare a document with all of your students' email addresses to share with the class. It is best to provide them with an online document that contains the emails so they can just copy and paste the email addresses when needed. This alleviates any spelling errors that can disrupt the process. An example form for this activity is shown in Figure 13-1.

Favorite Sports

Please answer all questions and click Submit. Thanks!
* Required

How much do you like to play sports? *
Please select an answer below.

1 2 3 4 5 6 7 8 9 10

Never ⦿○○○○○○○○ ○ As often as possible!

How often do you like to watch sports? *
Please choose one of the options below.

1 2 3 4 5 6 7 8 9 10

Not at all! ○○○○○○○○ ○ All the time!

Which is your favorite fall sport? *
Please pick one.

○ Football

○ Soccer

○ Volleyball

○ Golf

○ Field Hockey

○ Tennis

Which winter sports do you play or watch? *
You can check more than one!

☐ Basketball

☐ Ice Hockey

☐ Skiing/Snowboarding

☐ Wrestling

Which spring sport would you most likely play?
Choose one from the drop-down menu.

[⬍]

Submit

Never submit passwords through Google Forms.

Figure 13-1

Popular Sports Survey *(cont.)*

Activity 13

Procedure

1. Open a new form document in Google Docs.

2. At the top of the document in the **Untitled form** box, type "Favorite Sports" (Figure 13-2).

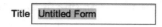

Figure 13-2

3. In the theme gallery, select the **Magazine** theme (Figure 13-3).

Figure 13-3

4. In the box below your form's title, type in the following directions: "Please answer all questions and click Submit. Thanks!"

5. Below the directions box is your first question. Click into the **Question Title** box and type in your first question: "How often do you like to play sports?" (Figure 13-4).

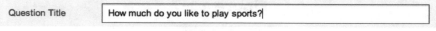

Figure 13-4

6. Next, click into the **Help Text** box and type "Please select an answer below."

7. Now use the **Question Type** drop-down menu and select **Scale** (Figure 13-5).

Figure 13-5

8. Next, use the **Scale** drop-down menus to set the scale from 1 to 10.

9. Click into the **1:** scale box and type "Never." Then click into the **10:** scale box and type "As often as possible!" (Figure 13-6).

Figure 13-6

10. Now put a check mark in the box next to **Required question**.

Popular
Sports Survey *(cont.)*

Activity 13

11. Click **Add item** to add another question.

12. Next you are going to create another scale question. Click into the **Question Title** box and type in your next question: "How often do you like to watch sports?"

13. Now under the **Help Text** box, type "Please choose one of the options below."

14. Next, click on the **Question Type** drop-down menu and choose the **Scale** option.

15. Set the scale to go from **1** to **10** using the drop-down menus.

16. Click into the **1:** label box and type "Not at all!"

17. Now click into the **10:** label box and type "All the time!"

18. Put a check mark in the **Required question** box, then click **Done**.

19. Next, you can add another question by clicking the **Add Item** button. Choose **Multiple choice** (Figure 13-7).

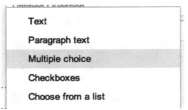

Figure 13-7

20. Now type your third question in the **Question Title** box: "Which is your favorite fall sport?"

21. Under the **Help Text** box, type "Please pick one."

22. Click into the **Option 1** box and type "Football." Then hit the **Enter** key on your keyboard to create an **Option 2** box (Figure 13-8).

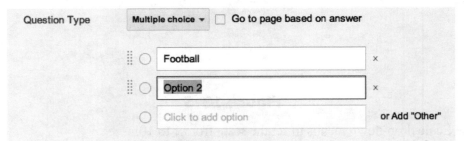

Figure 13-8

23. Type "Soccer" in the **Option 2** box, then hit the **Enter** key to add another choice: "Volleyball." To complete the possible answers, continue to add the following choices: "Golf," "Field Hockey," and "Tennis."

24. Put a check mark in the **Required question** box, then click **Done**.

25. Use the **Add Item** button to create a fourth question. This time choose **Checkboxes** from the **Question Type** drop-down menu.

26. In the **Question Title** box, type "Which winter sports do you play or watch?"

27. In the **Help Text** box, enter "You can check more than one!"

28. Click into the **Option 1** box and enter, **Basketball**. Click into the Option 2 box and type, **Ice Hockey**. For a third option type **Skiing/Snowboarding**. Finally add, **Wrestling** as a fourth option. (Figure 13-9).

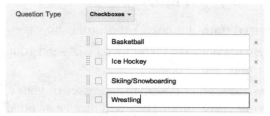

Figure 13-9

29. Make sure to check **Required question**, then click **Done**.

30. Finally, insert one last question into your form. Make this a **Choose from a list** question (Figure 13-10).

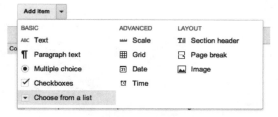

Figure 13-10

31. Enter the following in the **Question Title** box: "Which spring sport would you most likely play?"

32. In the **Help Text** box, type "Choose one from the drop-down menu."

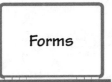

Forms

33. Click in to the Option **1** box and type "Baseball." Use Figure 13-11 to fill out the rest of the choices.

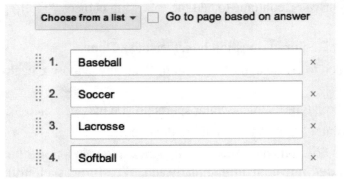

Figure 13-11

34. Put a check mark in the **Required question** box. Your form is now complete. Click the **Done** button.

35. Next, you will make a list of email contacts to whom you will send your questionnaire. Click on the **Send form** button at the top-right of your form.

36. In the **Send form via email** window, enter the email addresses of your classmates. Then click **Send**. Your form will now be emailed to your classmates. They will receive an email with a link to the form. You can click on the **See responses** button to view the results. Your project is now complete!

Favorite Animal

Activity 14

Objectives

Each student will utilize the Google Docs presentation application to create a presentation about his or her favorite animal.

Benchmarks for Technology Standards

Students will know the characteristics, uses, and basic features of computer software programs, including:

- using the common features of desktop publishing software (e.g., documents are created, designed, and formatted for publication; data and graphics can be imported into a document using desktop publishing software)

Learning Objectives

At the end of this lesson, students will be able to:

1. create a new presentation document
2. know the various terms associated with presentations including, slides, theme, slide show, normal view, title, and subtitle
3. select a theme for a presentation
4. insert a title into a presentation
5. insert a subtitle into a presentation
6. insert a bulleted list into a presentation
7. insert an image into a presentation
8. change the size of the font within a presentation
9. create a new slide within a presentation
10. view the presentation as a slide show
11. download the presentation in different formats

Before the Computer

This activity is written using the dolphin as the favorite animal, but you may choose to have your students research their own favorite animals prior to beginning this activity, and substitute them when creating their presentations. An example set of presentation slides for this activity is shown in Figure 14-1.

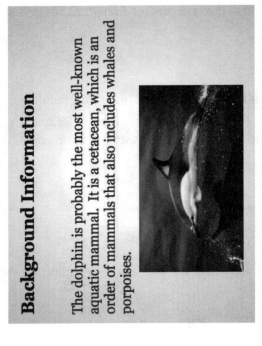

Background Information

The dolphin is probably the most well-known aquatic mammal. It is a cetacean, which is an order of mammals that also includes whales and porpoises.

Habitat

- Dolphins live all over the world, from warm coastal waters to the deep ocean. Some species of dolphins even live in freshwater rivers.
- They eat small fish, shrimp, crustaceans, and squid.

The Dolphin

My Favorite Animal
by Sam Student

Physical Appearance

- A dolphin can be gray, dark gray with white, or even black and white (orca).
- It breathes from a blowhole on top of its head.
- A dolphin has about 250 teeth with sharp tips that help to capture prey.
- It has a large, curved dorsal fin on its back.

Figure 14-1

Favorite Animal *(cont.)*

Activity 14

Procedure

1. Open a new presentation document in Google Docs.

2. First, you will set the theme for your presentation. A theme is a specific format for a presentation, which is applied to all slides. In the **Choose a theme** window that appears, click **Light Gradient** (Figure 14-2).

Figure 14-2

3. In the **Untitled Presentation** box, type your last name and "Dolphin."

4. Click into the **Click to add title** box and type "The Dolphin."

5. Next, click down into the **Click to add subtitle** box and type "My Favorite Animal."

6. Now hit the **Enter** key on your keyboard, type the word "by," and enter your first and last name (Figure 14-3).

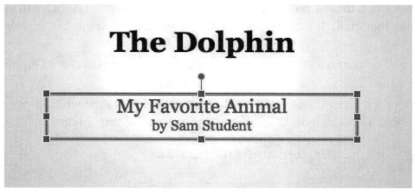

Figure 14-3

7. Next, click and drag over "by" and your name to highlight it. Then reduce its font size to **18 pt** using the **Font size** button (Figure 14-4).

Figure 14-4

Favorite Animal *(cont.)*

Presentations

Activity 14

8. Now go to the **Slide** menu and select **New slide** (Figure 14-5).

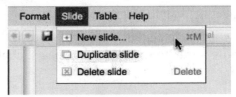

Figure 14-5

9. Go to the **Slide** menu again and choose **Change layout**. Select **Title and Body** (Figure 14-6).

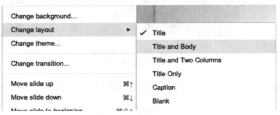

Figure 14-6

10. Your new slide should now have been inserted into your presentation. Click into the **Click to add title** box and type "Background Information."

11. Next, click into the **Click to add text** box and type in the following: "The dolphin is probably the most well-known aquatic mammal. It is a cetacean, which is an order of mammals that also includes whales and porpoises."

12. Once you have typed in your background information, click and drag over it to highlight it, then increase its font size to **26 pt**.

13. Next you will reduce the size of the text box to fit the text. Click on the white anchor point at the bottom corner of the text box, and drag it up to just below the last line of text (Figure 14-7).

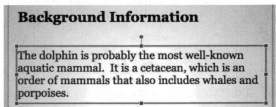

Figure 14-7

14. Next, you are going to insert an image on your slide just below the text box. There are two ways to insert images into a slide. First, you can select an image that is stored on your computer by choosing the **Insert** menu, and selecting **Image** (Figure 14-8).

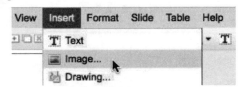

Figure 14-8

Favorite Animal *(cont.)*

Activity 14

15. You can then use the **Insert Image** window to navigate to the image file stored on your computer.

16. Another way to insert an image into a slide is to locate an image on a website, then just click and drag it onto your slide. To do this, go to the **File** menu of your web browser and choose **New Window** (Figure 14-9).

Figure 14-9

17. Next, navigate to the following web address: **http://www.google.com**. Click the **Image search** link at the top of the page, then type "dolphin" into the **Search Images** box and hit the **Search** button.

18. Your image search should have produced many images of dolphins. Click the bottom-corner of your web browser to minimize it so it takes up only half of your screen. Then click and drag an image of a dolphin onto your slide (Figure 14-10).

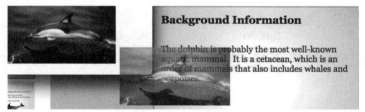

Figure 14-10

19. Your image should now be inserted into your slide. Click and drag the image so that it is positioned near the bottom-center of the slide. Use the anchor points to reduce its size so that it fits (Figure 14-11).

Figure 14-11

Favorite Animal *(cont.)*

Activity 14

20. Next, go to the **Slide** menu and choose **New slide**. Insert another **Title and Body** slide.

21. At the top of the slide, type "Physical Appearance." Click down to the **Click to add text** box. Now you are going to make your text appear as a list. Click the **Bullet list** button to begin the list (Figure 14-12).

Figure 14-12

22. Now type "A dolphin can be gray, dark gray with white, or even black and white (orca)." Hit the **Enter** key on your keyboard. Your bullet list should now continue.

23. On the next line, type "It breathes from a blowhole on top of its head." Add another line to your list and type "A dolphin has about 250 teeth with sharp tips that help to capture prey."

24. Hit **Enter** on your keyboard and add the last fact: "It has a large, curved dorsal fin on its back."

25. Using the same method as on the previous slide, insert an image into this slide and center it below the text.

26. Next, insert a new **Text** slide and add the following title: "Habitat."

27. Click down into the **Click to add text** box and create another bulleted list using the following information. On the first line, type "Dolphins live all over the world, from warm coastal waters to the deep ocean. Some species of dolphins even live in freshwater rivers." On the next line, type "They eat small fish, shrimp, crustaceans, and squid."

28. You can continue to add slides with more information if you have time.

29. To view your slide show, click the **Present** button located at the upper-right corner of your page (Figure 14-13).

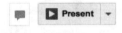

Figure 14-13

30. Your project is now complete! You can also download your presentation in different formats by selecting the **File** menu and choosing **Download As** (Figure 14-14).

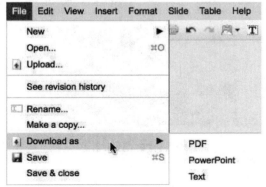

Figure 14-14

Invasive Species
Activity 15

Objectives

Each student will utilize the Google Docs presentation application to create a presentation about an invasive species that is disrupting North American ecosystems.

Benchmarks for Technology Standards

Students will know the characteristics, uses, and basic features of computer software programs, including:

- using the common features of desktop publishing software (e.g., documents are created, designed, and formatted for publication; data and graphics can be imported into a document using desktop publishing software)

Learning Objectives

At the end of this lesson, students will be able to:

1. create a new presentation document
2. know the various terms associated with presentations, including slides, theme, slide show, normal view, title, and subtitle
3. select a theme for a presentation
4. insert a title into a presentation
5. insert a subtitle into a presentation
6. insert a bulleted list into a presentation
7. insert an image into a presentation
8. insert a caption into a presentation
9. insert two columns into a presentation
10. change the size of the font within a presentation
11. create a new slide within a presentation
12. view the presentation as a slide show
13. download the presentation in different formats

Before the Computer

This activity is written using the zebra mussel as the invasive species, but you may choose to have your students research another invasive organism, and substitute it when creating their presentations. An example set of presentation slides for this activity is shown in Figure 15-1.

Invasive Species *(cont.)*

Activity 15

The Zebra Mussel

An Invasive Species
by Susan Student

What Is an Invasive Species?

An invasive species is an organism that is introduced into an ecosystem where it does not normally live, and where its presence causes harm.

The zebra mussel is a species of freshwater mollusk that has alternating stripes on its shell. It has become an invasive species in North America, Great Britain, Ireland, Italy, Spain, and Sweden.

Where Did It Come From?

The zebra mussel originates from the Caspian and Black Sea region of Asia.

It was transported to the Great Lakes region of North America in the ballast water of ships.

Why Is It Harmful?

The zebra mussel grows rapidly and can coat everything!

How Can It Be Controlled?

- using chemicals (like bleach) to kill it
- physical removal by scraping or high-pressure water
- using special paints and coatings to prevent its growth
- ultraviolet light
- using copper, brass, and galvanized metal pipes
- filters and screens
- electric currents
- biological controls (predators, diseases, parasites)

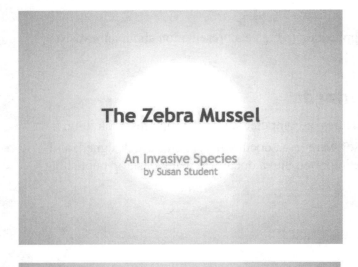

Figure 15-1

Invasive Species (cont.)

Activity 15

Procedure

1. Open a new presentation document in Google Docs.

2. First, you are going to set the theme for your presentation. A theme is a specific format for a presentation, which is applied to all slides. Select the **Light Gradient** theme (Figure 15-2).

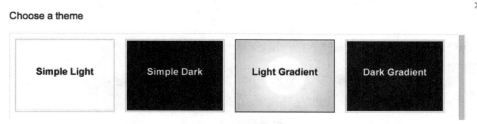

Figure 15-2

3. In the **Untitled Presentation** box, type your last name and "Invasive Species."

4. Click into the **Click to add title** box and type "The Zebra Mussel" (Figure 15-3).

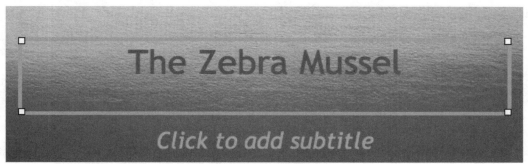

Figure 15-3

5. Next, click down into the **Click to add subtitle** box and enter "An Invasive Species."

6. Now hit the **Enter** key on your keyboard, type the word "by," and enter your first and last name (Figure 15-4).

Figure 15-4

Presentations

7. Next, click and drag over "by" and your name to highlight it. Then reduce its font size to **18 pt** using the **Font Size** button (Figure 15-5).

Figure 15-5

8. Now go to the **Slide** menu and select **New slide** (Figure 15-6).

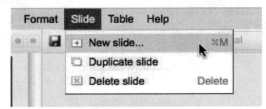

Figure 15-6

9. Go to the **Slide** menu again and select **Change Layout**. Select **Title and Body** (Figure 15-7).

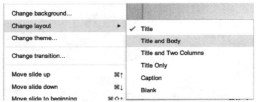

Figure 15-7

10. Your new slide should now have been inserted into your presentation. Click into the **Click to add title** box and type "What is an Invasive Species?"

11. Next, click into the **Click to add text** box and type in the following, "An invasive species is an organism that is introduced into an ecosystem where it does not normally live, and where its presence causes harm."

12. Now, click and drag over the text you just entered into your slide to highlight it, then click the **Center** align button (Figure 15-8).

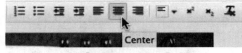

Figure 15-8

13. Click to the end of the sentence, then hit the **Enter** key on your keyboard twice to bring you down two lines. Now type "The zebra mussel is a species of freshwater mollusk that has alternating stripes on its shell. It has become an invasive species in North America, Great Britain, Ireland, Italy, Spain, and Sweden."

14. Next, you will insert an image into the slide. There are two ways to insert images into a slide. First, you can choose the **Insert** menu, then select **Image** (Figure 15-9). You can then use the **Insert Image** window to navigate to the image file stored on your computer.

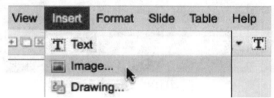

Figure 15-9

15. Another way to insert an image into your slide is to locate an image on a website, then click and drag it onto your slide. To do this, go to the **File** menu on your web browser and choose **New Window** (Figure 15-10).

Figure 15-10

16. Next, navigate to the following web address, **http://www.google.com**. Click the **Images** search link at the top of the page, type " Zebra Mussel" into the **Search Images** box, and hit the **Search** button.

17. Your image search should have produced many images of zebra mussels. Click the bottom corner of your web browser to minimize it so it takes up only half of your screen. Then click and drag an image of a zebra mussel onto your slide (Figure 15-11).

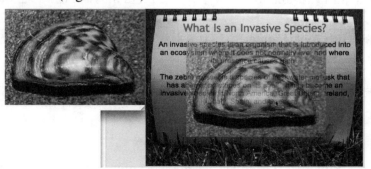

Figure 15-11

Invasive Species (cont.)
Activity 15

18. Your image should now be inserted into your slide. Click and drag the image so that it is positioned near the bottom-center of the slide. Use the anchor points to reduce the size so that it fits (Figure 15-14).

Figure 15-14

19. Next, go to the **Slide** menu and choose **New slide**. Change the layout to a **Title and Two Columns** slide (Figure 15-13).

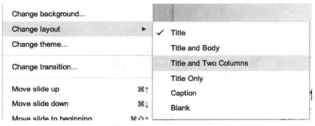

Figure 15-13

20. Click into the **Click to add title** box, and type "Where Did It Come From?"

21. Now click into the left-hand **Click to add content** box and type "The zebra mussel originates from the Caspian and Black Sea region of Asia."

22. Now click into the right-hand **Click to add content** box and type "It was transported to the Great Lakes region of North America in the ballast water of ships."

23. Insert another image of the zebra mussel at the bottom center of this slide.

24. Next, go to the **Slide** menu and choose **New Slide**. Make this one a **Caption** slide.

25. Click into the **Click to add caption** box and type "The zebra mussel grows rapidly and can coat everything!"

26. Next, click on the **Text box** tool (Figure 15-14). A text box should now appear in your slide.

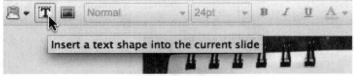

Figure 15-14

27. Type into the text box, "Why Is It Harmful?" Click the **Center** align button to center the text.

Invasive Species *(cont.)*
Activity 15

28. Highlight the text and increase its font size to **32 pt** using the **Font size** drop-down menu (Figure 15-15).

Figure 15-15

29. With the text still highlighted, change its color to a **light green** using the **Text color** tool (Figure 15-16).

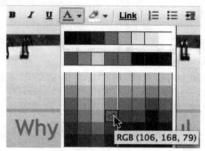

Figure 15-16

30. Finally, with the text still highlighted, change the font to **Trebuchet** using the **Font** drop-down menu (Figure 15-17).

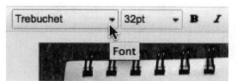

Figure 15-17

31. Next, click and drag the anchor point at the lower right of the text box to reduce its size so it fits around the text. Then click and drag it to the top center of the slide (Figure 15-18).

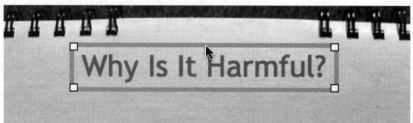

Figure 15-18

32. Next, search for an image of zebra mussels covering an object and insert it into your slide.

33. Now, go to the **Slide** menu and choose **New slide**. Insert a **Text** slide.

34. Click into the **Click to add title** box and type "How Can It Be Controlled?"

35. Next, click down to the **Click to add content** box.

36. Now you are going to make your text appear as a list. Click the **Bullet list** button (Figure 15-19).

Figure 15-19

37. Now type in the control methods shown in Figure 15-20 below.

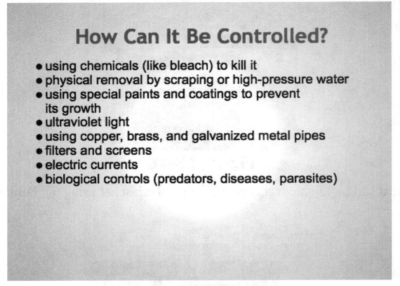

Figure 15-20

38. To view your slide show, click the **Present** button located at the top-right corner of your page (Figure 15-21).

Figure 15-21

39. Your project is now complete! You can also download your presentation in different formats by selecting the **File** menu and choosing **Download As** (Figure 15-22).

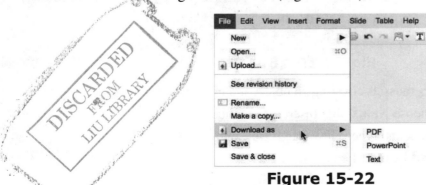

Figure 15-22